SCHOLASTIC

50 GRAPHIC ORGANIZERS FOR THE
Interactive Whiteboard

WHITEBOARD-READY GRAPHIC ORGANIZERS FOR READING, WRITING, MATH, AND MORE—TO MAKE LEARNING ENGAGING AND INTERACTIVE

by Jennifer Jacobson & Dottie Raymer
Illustrated by Amy Redmond

New York • Toronto • London • Auckland • Sydney
Mexico City • New Delhi • Hong Kong • Buenos Aires

Teaching *Resources*

Text © 2010, 1999 by Jennifer Jacobson and Dottie Raymer.
Illustrations © 2010, 1999 by Amy Redmond.

ISBN: 0-545-20715-0
10 9 8 7 6 5 4 3 2

*Special thanks to Lila Becker, Samantha Becker, Trevor Mayer,
Alex Steinberg, Emily Warne, Jenna Warne*

Edited by Lissa Wolfendale, Maria L. Chang, and Betsy Pringle
Design and illustrations by Amy Redmond
Production by Jennifer Marx

50 Graphic Organizers for the Interactive Whiteboard
is produced by **becker&mayer!**, Bellevue, WA

10886

Table of CONTENTS

Dear Teachers,

It is with great pleasure that we present *50 Graphic Organizers for the Interactive Whiteboard*. The graphic organizers in this book are the same tried-and-true teaching tools that we first introduced in our best-seller, *The Big Book of Reproducible Graphic Organizers*. With this new version, we've made these tools even easier for you and your students to use.

These graphic organizers remain as effective and as versatile as ever. However, technology has probably changed the landscape of your classroom. Perhaps you no longer use a chalkboard or an overhead projector. Instead, you connect wirelessly to a printer, flip on an LCD projector to display visuals, or use an interactive whiteboard to engage students.

To keep up with this technology, we are providing a companion CD that contains all of the graphic organizers in this book. The graphic organizers are in both PDF (Adobe Acrobat®) and Notebook (SMART Board®) formats. This way, you have the option of photocopying the reproducible pages in this book, printing them from the CD, or displaying them on your interactive whiteboard. Students can even work on the organizers independently at the computer center. They can fill out each organizer by hand or by typing in the interactive fields in the PDF versions*. In addition, after they've filled out the digital forms, they can save and print them. Using the graphic organizers has never been easier! And don't worry, even if you're still using the reliable overhead projector, the CD allows you to print directly onto transparencies.

We hope this electronic version makes teaching just a little bit easier. Perhaps it will entice you to try a new graphic organizer or use old favorites in new ways. We're amazed that even after years of experimenting with graphic organizers we're still making new connections— still finding new approaches for tapping into student thinking and promoting learning in meaningful ways.

Our very best wishes—

Jennifer and Dottie

TIP
To customize and save the PDF files on CD, you will need to download Adobe Reader, version 7.0 or higher. This download is available free of charge for Mac and PC systems at http://get. adobe.com/reader/.

*NOTE: The following graphic organizers do not contain interactive fields in the PDF format: What's the Main Idea? (page 25), Organizing Power (page 51), and Pieces of the Pie (page 85).

INTRODUCTION

Teaching has never been more exciting! Thoughtful educators everywhere are focusing on the importance of developing children's critical thinking skills. We know that *how* children learn, how they analyze and process information, is as important as *what* they learn. Graphic organizers are an invaluable teaching and learning tool that helps children to develop thinking strategies. They are visual representations that provide students with successful methods of organizing, interpreting, and understanding material.

Chances are you already have a few graphic organizers up your sleeve. Different forms of webs, maps, and diagrams have been passed from teacher to teacher like dog-eared treasure maps for years. Venn diagrams and Number Grids are staples of exemplary instruction. Here in *50 Graphic Organizers for the Interactive Whiteboard,* we've collected the best of those traditional models with a wide selection of new and creative formats to give you one definitive resource.

HOW THE BOOK IS DESIGNED

You will find the organizers divided into five areas: Language Arts, Social Studies, Science, Mathematics, and Study Skills. Left-hand pages provide directions on how to use the graphic organizer and two illustrations of ways in which teachers have used it at primary and intermediate grade levels. The bulleted list at the top of the left-hand page will help you see at a glance which skills you will be teaching, practicing, or assessing.

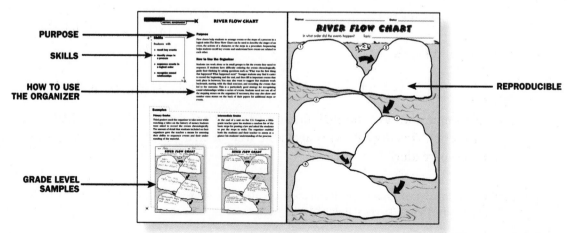

PURPOSE

SKILLS

HOW TO USE
THE ORGANIZER

GRADE LEVEL
SAMPLES

REPRODUCIBLE

HOW TO USE THE ORGANIZERS

The organizers in this book can be used with a whole class, small groups, or individual students. They are ideal for guiding cooperative learning groups or independent work at home. You can:

- View the organizer with the use of an interactive whiteboard, an LCD projector, or an overhead projector.
- Draw the organizer on a whiteboard or easel pad.
- Print organizers from the CD to hand out to students.
- Keep a supply of frequently used organizers on hand for students to use independently.

TEACHING TIPS

Graphic organizers have many purposes. They can be used for:

- Curriculum planning.
- Helping students process information.
- Pre- or post-assessment.

Here are a few suggestions on how to use graphic organizers in each of these ways.

Curriculum Planning

Before beginning a new unit or course of study, record children's prior knowledge with the use of graphic organizers. This can be done on an individual basis or as a whole group. For instance, if you wanted to introduce a unit on Living Organisms, you might display the Matrix organizer on your interactive whiteboard to elicit your students' knowledge of the classification of living things. By asking questions and recording student ideas, you can determine where gaps of understanding or mis- conceptions exist. You can then tailor your instruction and provide more learning experiences as needed.

With the use of graphic organizers, students can design their projects, too. They can plan stories, reports, and oral presentations. They can exercise prewriting skills and choose which strategy to use to solve a math problem.

Processing Information

In order to learn effectively, children need to be active learners. They need to ask questions, apply critical thinking skills, and develop a strong set of learning strategies. All of the graphic organizers in this book foster these skills. They can be presented to children individually, in small groups, or as a whole class.

In most instances, you will want to demonstrate how to use an organizer with large groups first. Have children take turns providing information and telling you where they would place it on the organizer. Model your own cognitive strategies by "thinking out loud." For example, while modeling the use of the Follow the Clues organizer (a graphic that helps children make predictions), you might say:

"When I read Ira Sleeps Over *and Reggie suggested they tell ghost stories, I predicted that Ira would want his teddy bear, so I'm going to write 'ghost stories' in this footprint."*

Graphic organizers provide the perfect opportunity for you to teach effective learning strategies. Encouraging individuals or small groups to complete graphic organizers at different stages of learning helps them to become engaged and stay engaged. When using a KWL chart, students remain active learners when reading nonfiction. They call on their background knowledge to create necessary "hooks" for new learning. When using the Climbing the Mountain organizer, students keep an organizational structure in mind as they do research. They are better able to determine which pieces of information are the important facts and which are minor details. When using the Star Solver organizer, children practice the steps of problem solving and perhaps consider a new way of approaching a math problem. Introduce these organizers at the beginning of a project and have children return to them frequently to add information they've acquired.

Graphic organizers are also excellent tools for helping children to work together cooperatively. They encourage the expression of ideas, the making of connections, and worthwhile discussion. Children who are auditory learners get the added benefit of "hearing" how information can be classified. Most teachers have found that children who are taught to follow a process for working together gain valuable social skills as well as a greater comprehension of the material. Here is one teacher's posted list of procedures:

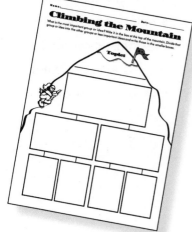

- Listen to everyone's ideas.

- Question others to understand their thinking.

- Point out what works.

- Agree on an approach.

- Share your results.

Assessment

Graphic organizers allow you to assess a child's understanding at a glance. You can use the graphic organizers in this book to determine the depth of a student's understanding—the connections that have been made. For instance, after the study of plant life, you could use the Focus on a Cycle organizer to determine whether your students have grasped an understanding of how plants are an important element of food cycles. You might provide some of the key words and suggest that they supply the rest.

Children can also use graphic organizers to assess their own learning. After writing a story, for example, a student could complete the Build a Story organizer. While completing the graphic, the student would need to ask him- or herself: Did I create an identifiable setting? Did I give my character(s) a problem? Did I come up with a successful solution?

Graphic organizers are a performance-based model of assessment and are ideal for including in student portfolios, since they require students to demonstrate both their grasp of the concepts and their reasoning.

Students who receive plenty of practice with graphic organizers recognize their value. They begin to draw them on their own to explore ideas. A child, for instance, who is preparing to write a personal essay might begin by recording his or her ideas on a web. The child who is trying to figure out the greatest common factor of a number might draw a Venn diagram. When your children have reached this level of sophisticated learning, you might suggest that they draw a graphic organizer of their choice to demonstrate what they have learned about a particular subject. You may want to provide them with key words for optimum results.

KEEPING TEACHERS IN MIND

Whether you are a teacher who has been using graphic organizers for years, or just beginning, this book has been designed for you. We hope that *50 Graphic Organizers for the Interactive Whiteboard* will save you time and meet the specific needs of your program. You will probably find that you can take our ideas as springboards for your own. For instance, our graphic organizer for sorting spelling words has laundry baskets. If you find this graphic particularly useful to you, you and your students might design your own graphic to tie in with a particular theme—thereby taking learning one step further. When your students decide to categorize their pond life vocabulary words in aquariums, for instance, they are learning a tool for making their own learning connections. You will find, time and time again, that creating and using visual representations leads to greater comprehension of material and recall. Best wishes as you and your students make new discoveries.

 # THE ORGANIZERS

CAUSE-EFFECT CONTRAPTION

Skills

Students will:

+ **identify causes and effects within stories**

+ **analyze causal relationships**

+ **recognize consequences of characters' actions**

Purpose

Identifying cause and effect relationships within a story helps students focus on two important elements of comprehension: *what* happened in the story, and *why* it happened. Looking for causes and their effects gives students an opportunity to look carefully at the consequences of characters' actions and to think about how different actions might have different effects.

How to Use the Organizer

Introduce the Cause-Effect Contraption. Point out that in each machine the marble rolling down the tube is about to *cause* something to happen. Ask what the *effect* of the rolling marble will be. (The dominoes will be knocked over.) Explain that in stories, "what happens" is often the *effect* of an action or event and "why it happened" is the event's *cause*.

Suggest students choose a character's action from a story and write a brief description of the action in the space labeled *Cause*. Then ask them to think about the results of that action and record the consequences under *Effect*. In some cases, students may find it easier first to describe an event or action under *Effect* and then record why the event happened under *Cause*. Be sure to point out that one cause may have a number of different effects and that one effect may have many different causes.

Examples

Primary Grades

After reading *Jiro's Pearl* by Daniel Powers, second-grade students worked in small groups to identify two important actions taken by the main character. By recording the actions and the results of those actions, they were able to see that a character's actions can have either positive or negative effects.

Intermediate Grades

While reading Avi's *Nothing But the Truth,* a sixth-grade class discussed the causes of Phillip's suspension from school and the subsequent national uproar. Students recorded a number of possible causes for each event so that they could better analyze the events and come up with their own versions of "the truth."

CAUSE-EFFECT CONTRAPTION

Put each Cause-Effect Contraption into action. Write a cause inside the box of marbles.
Write its effect within the ring of dominoes.

CAUSE

EFFECT

CAUSE

EFFECT

FOLLOW THE CLUES

Skills

Students will:

+ **predict the outcome of a story**

+ **identify clues leading to an outcome**

+ **draw conclusions based on clues in a story**

Purpose

Making and then confirming or revising predictions helps readers to stay fully engaged in a story. As readers develop this skill, they use clues from the story and their own lives to predict how characters will behave and how key problems in the story will be solved. This organizer helps students identify clues in a story that will help them make reasonable predictions.

How to Use the Organizer

Introduce the Follow the Clues organizer by asking how detectives go about solving mysteries. (They look for clues and draw conclusions from the clues.) Discuss how readers also use clues to help them make sense of what they are reading. Encourage students to predict how a story they are currently reading will end or how a major problem in the story will be solved. Suggest that they write their predictions on the door labeled "prediction." As students read, encourage them to record clues that either support or refute their prediction. If necessary, allow students to revise their predictions to reflect the clues they have found in the text.

Examples

Primary Grades

While reading *Ira Sleeps Over* aloud, a first-grade teacher asked her students to predict whether or not Ira would want to take his teddy bear on a sleepover. As she read the story aloud, she asked students to suggest clues from the book that helped them make their predictions.

Intermediate Grades

A fourth grader chose *Stone Fox* as an independent reading book. During reading conferences, the teacher asked him to predict the ending of the story. The student then completed the graphic organizer by filling in clues as he read. After he finished the book, he reviewed the clues and evaluated his prediction with the teacher.

Follow the Clues

Can you predict what will happen next? Write the clues on
the footsteps. Then write your prediction on the door.

Clue

Clue

Clue

Prediction

STORY BOARD

✦ Skills

Students will:

+ **recall story events**

+ **identify key events**

+ **sequence events in logical order**

Purpose

This graphic organizer helps students to arrange events in chronological order. It's useful for the exploration and discussion of story structure (i.e. beginning, middle, and end), cause and effect, and the varied ways in which authors work with time. The combination of visual images and text helps students to isolate key events.

How to Use the Organizer

It is useful for students, when first introduced to the Story Board organizer, to tell the events they have chosen to illustrate. You may want to invite students to talk in pairs, small groups, or with you in a reading conference. Some students will be able to tell the events in chronological order. Others, particularly readers of chapter books, may find it easier to tell the beginning, the end, and then go back and isolate important events that occurred in the middle. Let students know that this is a particularly good strategy, for it helps them recognize the specific events that led to the conclusion. Once students have talked as a prewriting activity, encourage them to complete the organizer. Students may also want to use this organizer to plan their own stories.

Examples

Primary Grades

A first-grade student chose to illustrate the events of "The Three Billy Goats Gruff." Later, he used his Story Board to retell the story to a classmate.

Intermediate Grades

A fourth-grade student explored the author's literary technique—using a flashback—as she retold the story of *Crossing the Starlight Bridge* by Alice Mead.

Name: _____ Date: _____

Book Title: _____ Author: _____

STORY BOARD

Draw or write the events of the story on the story board. Record them in the correct order.

1

2

3

4

5

6

KWL

Purpose

Activating background knowledge, creating questions about the topic, and developing a purpose for reading help students to become more thoughtful, engaged readers. The KWL organizer guides students through this three-step process—a process they can add to their list of comprehension strategies.

How to Use the Organizer

Before reading, ask students to record what they know about the topic in the first column. Then, have them list questions that they hope the book or article will answer. Tell them that, as they read, they may come up with new questions they hope will be answered, and they can add these to the W column. After students finish reading, have them record what they've learned in the L column. Explain that one book or article may not answer *all* their questions. Help them to find new resources that may.

✦✦ Skills

Students will:

✦ recall their background knowledge

✦ identify a reading purpose

✦ record new content knowledge

Examples

Primary Grades

For independent reading time, a second grader selected the book *Whales: The Gentle Giants* by Joyce Milton. Instead of writing an entry in his reading log, he chose to complete a KWL chart as he read. This is just one of the many options his teacher had made available for responding to books.

Intermediate Grades

Each week, fifth graders were asked to complete a KWL chart while reading about a current event in the local newspapers. The charts helped students to develop their own purpose for reading newspapers and to organize their thoughts before presenting information to the class.

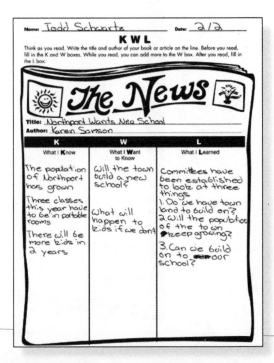

Name: _____   Date: _____

K W L

Think as you read. Write the title and author of your book or article on the line. Before you read, fill in the K and W boxes. While you read, you can add more to the W box. After you read, fill in the L box.

The News

Title: _____
Author: _____

K	W	L
What I **K**now	What I **W**ant to Know	What I **L**earned

COMPARING CHARACTERS

✦ Skills

Students will:

✦ **recognize character traits**

✦ **compare and contrast two characters**

✦ **make judgments regarding similarities and differences**

Purpose

The Comparing Characters Venn diagram helps students to compare character traits and make literary connections. They can use the organizer to compare two characters from the same story, characters from two different stories, or to compare and contrast a literary character with an actual person.

How to Use the Organizer

Model the use of this graphic organizer by comparing and contrasting two well-known literary characters. Write the names of the characters inside the hats. Then have students supply character traits. Write differences in the outer circles. If the characters share a trait, show students how to record the information in the place where the circles overlap.

Examples

Primary Grades

A group of second graders compared and contrasted the wolves from the stories "The Three Little Pigs" and "Little Red Riding Hood."

Intermediate Grades

Fifth-grade students were asked to compare two characters from a novel as part of their final assessment on historical fiction. This student chose to describe two characters from *Bat 6* by Virginia Euwer Wolff.

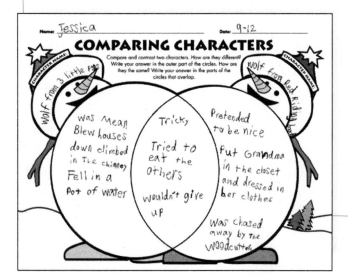

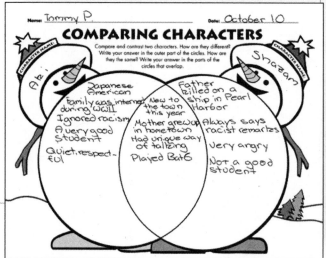

Name: _____

Date: _____

COMPARING CHARACTERS

Compare and contrast two characters. How are they different? Write your answer in the outer part of the circles. How are they the same? Write your answer in the parts of the circles that overlap.

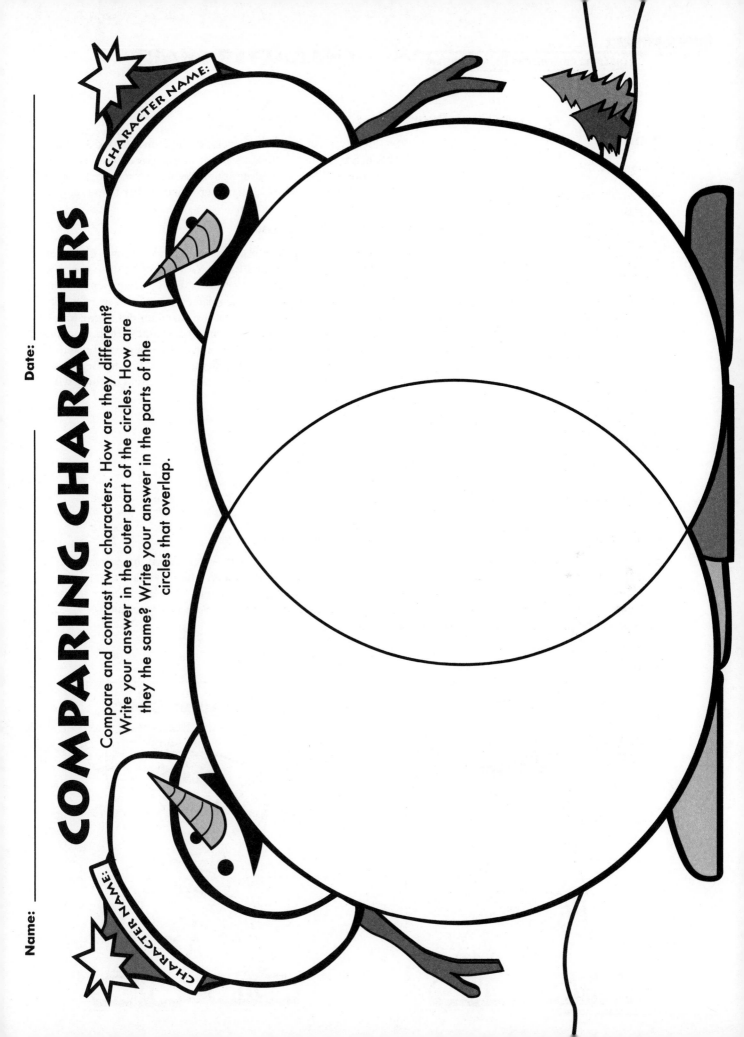

CHARACTER NAME:

CHARACTER NAME:

CHARACTER CHART

Skills

Students will:

+ **identify character traits**

+ **infer character traits from story clues**

+ **show character through action in their writing**

Purpose

Most often, literary characters are developed and understood by their actions. This organizer helps students to see the connection between a character's actions and his or her description. Used as a prewriting tool, it helps students to "show what their character is like," rather than telling.

How to Use the Organizer

Model the use of this organizer using a well-known literary character. Write the name of the character on the face. Next, ask students to describe the character to you. As the class offers adjectives, record them on the tummy and ask, "How do you know the character is (mean, smart, tricky, etc.)?" Encourage students to tell you what the character did to create this impression. Record the character's actions on the limbs. Help students understand that good writers show their readers, through a character's behavior, what a character is like. (If students have difficulty beginning with the description, they may write actions first and later conclude what those actions tell about the character.)

Examples

Primary Grades

After a third grader wrote a story, she used the Character Chart to determine whether she had shown readers what her character, Polly, was like. Realizing that she hadn't demonstrated that Polly was sneaky, she returned to her story to add a part.

Intermediate Grades

Sixth-grade students were asked to demonstrate how friendship, rather than increased prejudice, grew through the actions of one character in the book *The Storyteller's Beads* by Jane Kurtz.

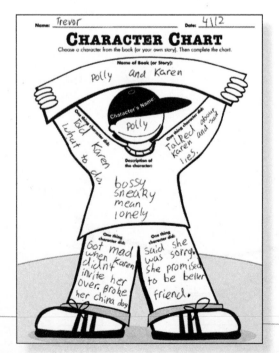

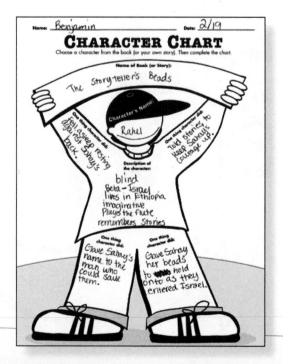

Name: _____ Date: _____

CHARACTER CHART

Choose a character from the book (or your own story). Then complete the chart.

Name of Book (or Story):

Character's Name:

One thing character did:

One thing character did:

Description of the character:

One thing character did:

One thing character did:

WHAT'S THE MAIN IDEA?

✦ Skills

Students will:

✦ **determine the main idea of an article**

✦ **identify supporting details**

✦ **recognize extraneous information**

Purpose

The fishbone organizer helps students recognize that nonfiction articles and expository writing contain a main idea and supporting details. As they isolate specific information to record on the organizer, students make decisions regarding its relevance, thereby increasing their understanding that not all text is of equal importance. Students who are writing essays or articles can use the graphic during prewriting to ensure that their work contains a main idea and to help them develop a structure for their piece.

How to Use the Organizer

After reading an article, have students determine the main idea and write it on the spine of the fish. Then encourage them to write the details that support the main idea inside the divisions made by the other bones. Students who wish to use the graphic organizer to plan their own writing can begin with the main idea or record facts first, which may lead them to the development of a main idea.

Examples

Primary Grades

After reading an article from their weekly news magazine, second graders helped their teacher complete the What's the Main Idea organizer on the interactive whiteboard.

Intermediate Grades

A small group of fourth graders used What's the Main Idea? to organize an article they were composing for the school newspaper.

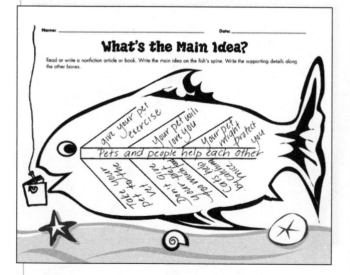

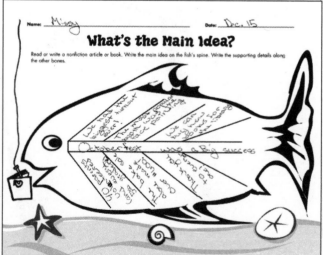

Name: _____

What's the Main idea?

Read or write a nonfiction article or book. Write the main idea on the fish's spine. Write the supporting details along the other bones.

EDITOR'S CHECKLIST

Skills

Students will:

+ apply their knowledge of punctuation, spelling, and grammar

+ identify effective writing techniques

+ edit their own written work

Purpose

Editing one's own written work can be an overwhelming task. This organizer helps students recall specific skills that they've been introduced to, and are ready to incorporate in their writing. As students use the checklist, they can reinforce their knowledge of punctuation, spelling, grammar, and writing techniques. Or they can use the checklist to make sure they've met all the criteria for a particular assignment.

How to Use the Organizer

For individual use: Keep a steady supply of organizers in the classroom. As you inform students about their writing, point out the skills that you would like them to edit on a regular basis. Have them record these skills on the left-hand side of the checklist. When they are ready to edit a piece, have them write the title of the written work at the top and then look to make sure that each skill recorded has been applied.

For whole class use: Encourage students to record the criteria for a particular writing assignment on the left-hand side of the organizer. Later, when editing their final work, they can use the checklist to ensure that all criteria have been met.

Examples

Primary Grades

Second graders kept a copy of the Editor's Checklist in their writing folder. When they completed a story, they used the checklist to do a preliminary edit of their own writing. As they learned and demonstrated new skills, such as capitalizing proper nouns, they added that skill to their checklist.

Intermediate Grades

Asked to write articles for the class newspaper, fifth graders recorded the assigned criteria on an Editor's Checklist. When editing their work, they reviewed the list to make sure their articles met all of the requirements.

Editor's Checklist

Be your own editor. Write the skills you know down the side. Write the title of your work at the top. Edit your writing, checking off the skills as you go.

Skills I know and want to practice:

BUILDING A STORY

Purpose

All stories have common elements—problem, solution, characters, and setting. Story mapping is an effective way to help students use the structure of a story to organize their ideas before writing.

How to Use the Organizer

To introduce the organizer, review the elements of a story—problem, solution, characters, and setting. Discuss how writers use these elements to "build" the structure of their story, much as carpenters use building materials to build the structure of a house.

Suggest that students use the organizer to brainstorm ideas for an original story. As students think about the elements they want to include in their stories, show them how to record their ideas in the appropriate spaces. Students can use their organizers as guides as they write their stories.

Examples

Primary Grades

A first-grade teacher used the organizer to record ideas for a class story about a trip to a roller-skating rink. The organizer helped students identify missing information and visualize individual pieces of information fitting together to form a story.

Intermediate Grades

A fifth grader used the organizer to plan an original story about a girl living during the American Revolution. As she brainstormed ideas for her story, she recorded each one in the appropriate space on the organizer and thought about which elements would fit together to make the strongest story. She then circled the elements she wanted in her story and used the organizer as a guide as she wrote the story.

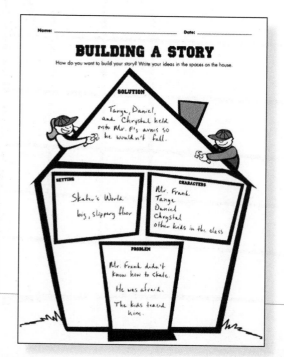

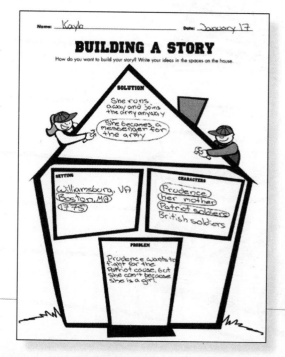

Name: _____   Date: _____

BUILDING A STORY

How do you want to build your story? Write your ideas in the spaces on the house.

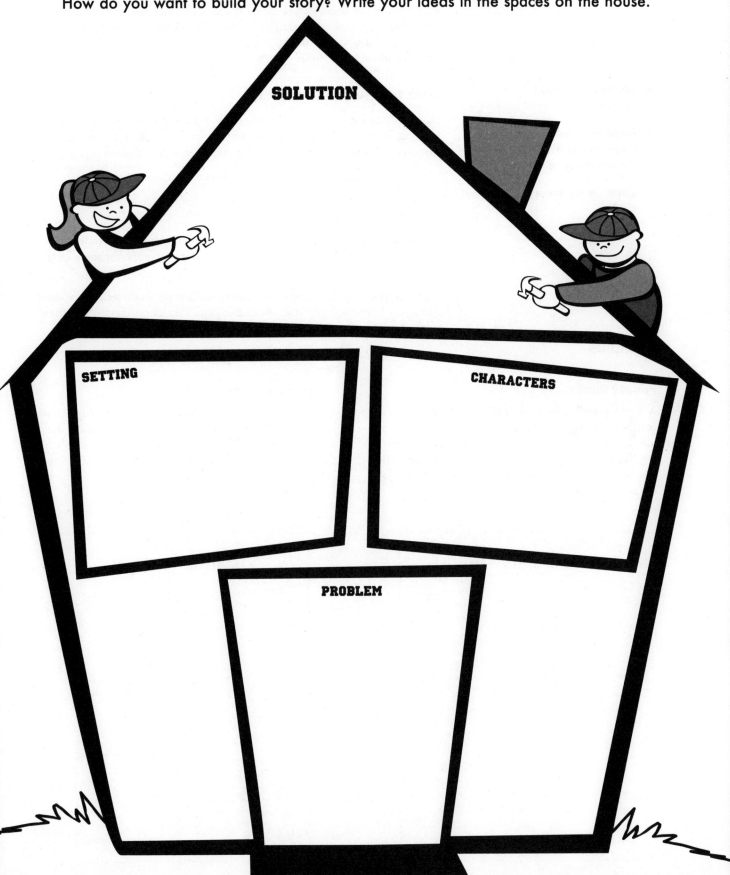

SOLUTION

SETTING

CHARACTERS

PROBLEM

VOCABULARY QUILT

Skills

Students will:

+ **recall background knowledge**

+ **identify unfamiliar words**

+ **focus on context clues to determine the meaning of words**

+ **practice dictionary skills**

Purpose

The Vocabulary Quilt organizer helps children to identify new vocabulary and encourages them to use context clues to determine the meaning of the word—an essential strategy for reading comprehension. When the meaning of the word cannot be determined from the text, children gain practice in using dictionary skills.

How to Use the Organizer

Demonstrate the use of this organizer by modeling how you would select a word, search for context clues, and record the inferred meaning. For instance, after identifying a new word, show students how to:

• predict the meaning of the word from what came before, or

• read on a little ways and then reread the sentence with the new vocabulary word.

When inferring the meaning of the word, "think aloud" so students can hear your process, or identify clue words that indicate the meaning of the new word.

You may also want to review dictionary skills with students if necessary. After you have modeled the use of the organizer, children can use them while reading with the whole class, small groups, or independently.

Examples

Primary Grades

A third grader chose to read "Iron Hans" by the Brothers Grimm during a unit on fairy tales. She identified unfamiliar words and inferred their meaning from context clues. At her teacher's request, she put a star next to those words that she had to look up in the dictionary.

Intermediate Grades

A fourth-grade student read *Professor IQ Explores the Brain* by Seymour Simon and completed the Vocabulary Quilt as part of his book report. The organizer was particularly helpful in reinforcing the understanding of highly specific content words.

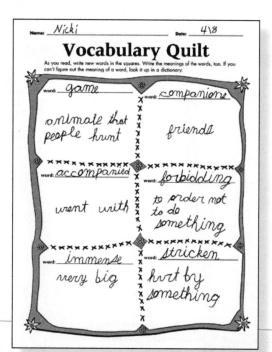

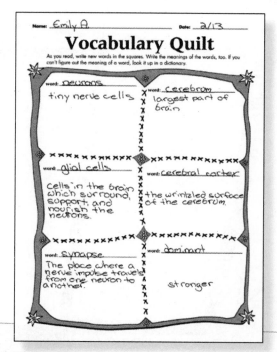

Vocabulary Quilt

As you read, write new words in the squares. Write the meanings of the words, too. If you can't figure out the meaning of a word, look it up in a dictionary.

word: _____

word: _____

word: _____

word: _____

word: _____

word: _____

SPELLING SORT

Skills

Students will:

+ **recognize spelling patterns**

+ **classify words according to common elements**

+ **strengthen visual memory**

Purpose

Visual discrimination is the ability to note similarities and differences among visual images and to retain what one has seen in the past. Good spellers often have strong visual memories—a skill which serves them well because so many words in English do not follow phonemic rules. As students sort spelling or vocabulary words, they analyze words for similar patterns and form their own visual connections, strengthening their powers of visual discrimination in the process.

How to Use the Organizer

Students can use this organizer to sort and organize formal lists of spelling words, content-area vocabulary, or personal "spelling demons." To introduce the organizer, write a list of words and draw a large laundry basket on the chalkboard. Discuss with students various ways of sorting the words in the list—by common phonemic or structural elements, for example. Record similar words inside the basket and write the sorting rule or category below. Suggest that students analyze their own lists of words to sort into different baskets on the organizer. Remind them that they do not have to use all of the baskets on the page, and that they can draw additional baskets on the back of the page if necessary. Discuss with students ideas for accommodating words that don't fit into any of their chosen categories, such as a "Misfits" or "Extras" basket.

Examples

Primary Grades

This third grader sorted a spelling list of words with the long *i* sound. Sorting the words helped him distinguish between different spellings for the same sound. Because he used the organizer to study for his weekly spelling test, he was able to visualize each word as part of a group having the same spelling pattern.

Intermediate Grades

As part of a vocabulary lesson, small groups of sixth graders brainstormed lists of words that contained prefixes. Students analyzed the structure of the words and classified them according to the meaning of their prefixes.

Spelling Sort

Sort your spelling words. In each basket, write words that are alike. Then write the sorting rule on the lines beneath the basket.

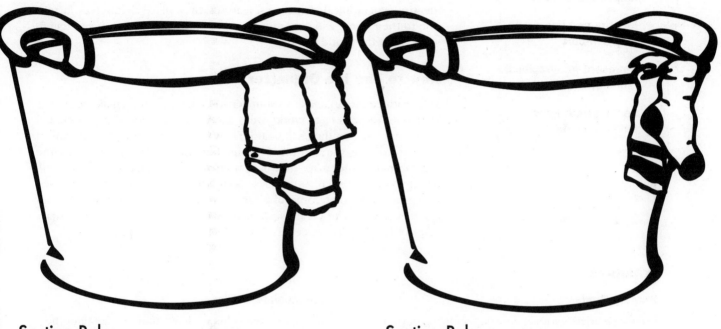

Sorting Rule: _____

_____

Sorting Rule: _____

_____

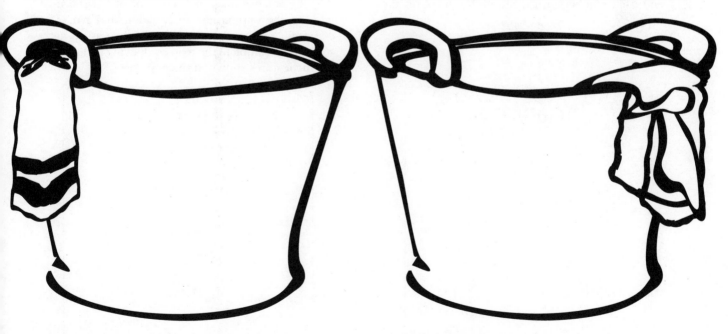

Sorting Rule: _____

_____

Sorting Rule: _____

_____

MAP IT OUT

✦ Skills

Students will:

✦ **understand key mapping concepts**

✦ **identify and use map symbols**

✦ **represent geographical landmarks on a map**

✦ **demonstrate knowledge of scale**

Purpose

Geographical knowledge—an understanding of the earth's natural features and human beings' relationship to those features—is essential to the study of the social sciences. One of the best ways for students to become familiar with the spatial forms and relationships that form the basis of geography is to participate in mapping activities. As students draw and identify geographical shapes and features, they place themselves in relation to their home and community and cultivate an interest in and understanding of the world at large.

How to Use the Organizer

To introduce the organizer to younger students, choose a small area of the classroom (a pet's cage works well) and have students help you draw a map of the area on the chalkboard. Draw a key for your map, and explain its purpose. For older students, point out the similarities between the organizer and other maps they have used. Younger students can map familiar surroundings such as the classroom, the schoolyard, or their houses, using numbers, colors, or symbols to create a map key. Older students can use the organizer to create scale maps of their surroundings, or to draw maps of less familiar places studied in history or geography lessons.

Examples

Primary Grades

Second graders worked in cooperative groups to create maps of their school playground. They decided on symbols to represent each piece of playground equipment, drew them in their relative positions, and used numbers to explain each symbol on the map key.

Intermediate Grades

In order to assess his students' understanding of the geography of their home state, a fourth-grade teacher gave each student the organizer with the outline of the state and the map key already filled in. (To do this, the teacher made one copy of the organizer, filled in the outline and information, and ran off copies for each of the students.) He then asked his students to complete the map by drawing and labeling the features shown in the key.

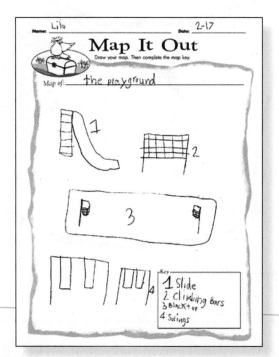

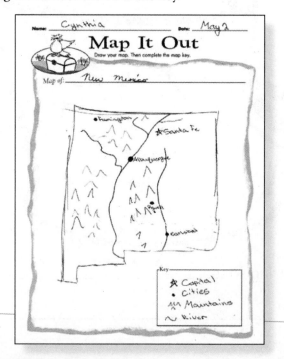

Map It Out

Draw your map. Then complete the map key.

Map of: _____

┌─Key────────────────────────┐
│   │
│   │
│   │
│   │
│   │
│   │
└────────────────────────────┘

ON THE ROAD TO THE FUTURE

Skills

Students will:

+ identify key events

+ sequence events in a logical order

+ place a series of events along a continuum of time

Purpose

Sequencing events helps students gain a sense of order and time. As students place key events, ideas, or people they are studying in a chronological sequence, they are better able to evaluate the information and form connections between the past and the present. This organizer provides students with a means for visualizing a sequence of events and gives them individualized practice in using and reading time lines.

How to Use the Organizer

Help students brainstorm and list key events in the time period they are studying. Then show them how to make one mark along the center line of the Road to the Future for each of the events in the list. Students can use words, pictures, or a combination of the two to label each mark. Ask volunteers to use their completed organizers to recall and retell the sequence of events that they have recorded.

Examples

Primary Grades

For a homework assignment, a first grader asked his father to help him list important events for each year of his life, beginning with his birth. Together, the student and his father chose one major event to highlight for each year, and decided how to mark and label the time line on the organizer. The father recorded the words for each label, and the student illustrated each event. At school, the student used the organizer to give a brief oral presentation about his life.

Intermediate Grades

Fifth graders studying the American Revolution used the organizer as a study aid for a unit test. The class first listed the major events of the Revolution on the chalkboard and discussed the significance of each event. Students recorded key events in order, and used the organizer to help them recall the events as they studied for the test.

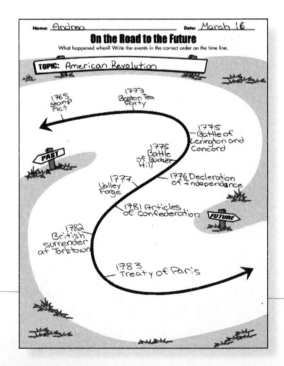

On the Road to the Future

What happened when? Write the events in the correct order on the time line.

TOPIC:

PAST

FUTURE

WINDOW FRAMES

✦ Skills

Students will:

✦ compare different times or cultures

✦ distinguish among different geographic and political regions

✦ identify key characteristics of cultures, places, events, or ideas

Purpose

Students can use this matrix to classify information by categories or characteristics. Organizing information in this way encourages students to use vocabulary associated with different times, places, and cultures. As students compare the classifications, they delineate similarities and differences and form connections among the subjects.

How to Use the Organizer

In the first column along the left side of the organizer, have students list the subjects that they wish to compare. Help them brainstorm specific categories or characteristics about the subjects, and write the categories in the squares across the top of the chart. Use completed charts as a basis for comparing and contrasting different cultures, events, places, or times.

Examples

Primary Grades

After reading *If You Sailed on the Mayflower* by Ann McGovern, a class of first graders brainstormed ways that the lives of the Pilgrims at Plymouth Plantation were the same as or different from their own lives. The teacher used the graphic organizer to record the class's conclusions.

Intermediate Grades

Fifth graders were asked to choose four states and do research to find each state's capital, largest city, land area, population, and the date that it entered the Union. Students used the graphic organizer to record and organize their findings. The comparisons in the matrix gave students a basis for choosing one state for future independent research.

Name: _____   Date: _____

Window Frames

Use these frames to make comparisons. In the frames along the side, write the items you want to compare. In the frames at the top, write the characteristics of the items that you want to compare. Then fill in the information.

	cooking	water	food	school
Pilgrims	fireplace	from a creek	hunted or grow it	learned at home
Us	stove	from a faucet	buy it at a store	go to school

Name: Alexander B.   Date: December 2, 1998

Window Frames

Use these frames to make comparisons. In the frames along the side, write the items you want to compare. In the frames at the top, write the characteristics of the items that you want to compare. Then fill in the information.

	Capital	largest city	Area (sq. miles)	Population
Alaska	Juneau	Anchorage	570,374	604,000
Washington	Olympia	Seattle	66,582	5,431,000
Oregon	Salem	Portland	96,003	3,141,000
California	Sacramento	Los Angeles	155,973	31,589,000

Window Frames

Use these frames to make comparisons. In the frames along the side, write the items you want to compare. In the frames at the top, write the characteristics of the items that you want to compare. Then fill in the information.

COAT OF ARMS

✦ Skills

Students will:

✦ identify characteristics of a person, place, or time period

✦ collect and organize information

✦ use vocabulary associated with different times, places, or events

Purpose

Social and historical knowledge is built upon an understanding of the distinguishing characteristics of the places, people, and times that make up the context of important events. To use this organizer, students collect, evaluate, and record information about a topic's important attributes—all important skills that lead to historical understanding.

How to Use the Organizer

To use this organizer as a research tool, have older students select and research a topic of their choice. As students arrange and classify their information into subtopics, they can write key attributes or facts in each of the four sections of the coat of arms. Younger students can draw pictures or write words or phrases describing the major traits or events of a topic they are currently studying. Display the Coats of Arms on a bulletin board or have students use them as study aids for writing reports or preparing for a test.

Examples

Primary Grades

First-grade students studying Martin Luther King, Jr. used the organizer to record what they had learned about his life and work. In each section of the Coat of Arms, students drew one picture representing an important character trait or event in King's life. The teacher helped the students label their drawings and asked volunteers to talk about the information they chose to portray on the Coats of Arms.

Intermediate Grades

Sixth graders were asked to report on an ancient civilization of their choice. After students researched their topics, they used the organizer as a prewriting aid to help them organize the information into four subtopics and recorded each topic and accompanying details in a section on the Coat of Arms. As students wrote their reports, they used the organizer to structure their writing.

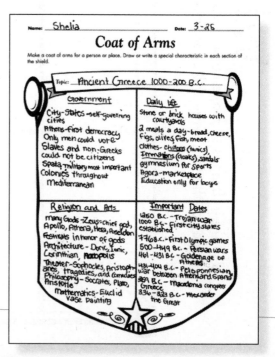

Coat of Arms

Make a coat of arms for a person or place. Draw or write a special characteristic in each section of the shield.

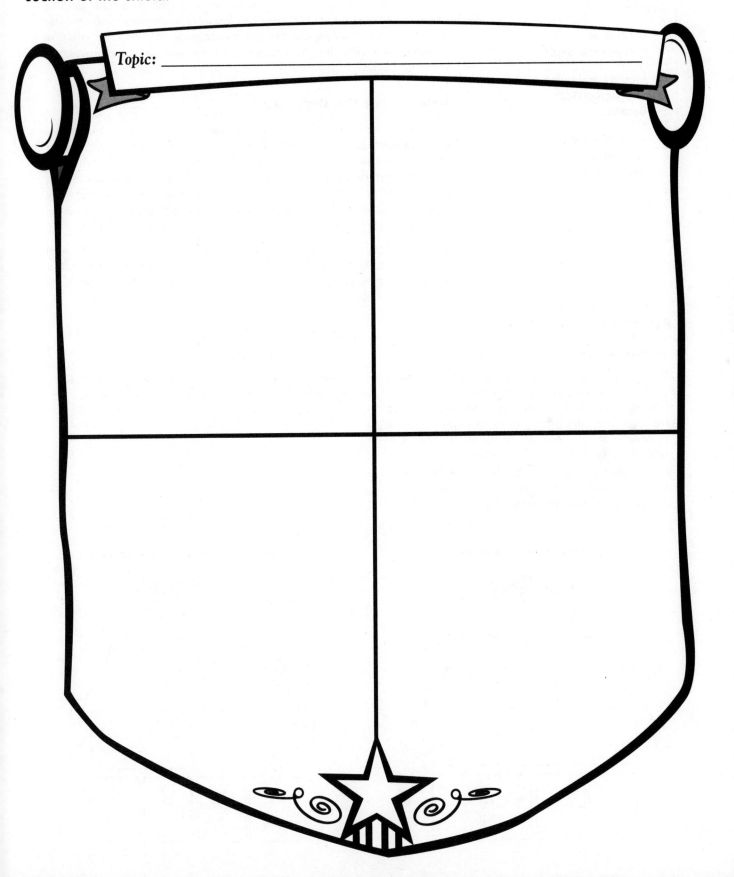

Topic: _____

CLIMBING THE MOUNTAIN

Skills

Students will:

+ **determine hierarchical order**

+ **identify main idea and supporting details**

+ **rank information in order of importance**

Purpose

Recognizing order of importance is a life skill that can help students establish priorities both in their studies and in their daily lives. This graphic organizer gives students the means to organize information and evaluate its importance. Students can use this organizer to help them to visualize hierarchical relationships, to categorize information, or to set personal or classroom goals.

How to Use the Organizer

If students are recording hierarchical information, such as the fourth-grade example below, instruct them to place the most important item at the top and work their way down the mountain in order of importance. You may need to use prompts such as "What's the most important idea of this article?" or "Who's the top dog here?" Let students know that they need not use all of the boxes in the organizer, and that they can divide boxes in order to accommodate additional information if necessary.

To use the organizer as a goal-setting or problem-solving tool, write the goal or problem in the box at the top. Record two ideas for reaching the goal or solving the problem, and then add details about each idea in the small boxes at the bottom of the mountain.

Examples

Primary Grades

Second graders used the organizer to help them plan a trip to the local children's museum. The class brainstormed ideas about what was needed and then divided into small groups to complete their organizers. As the groups shared their organizers with the class, the teacher recorded their ideas in a large organizer on the chalkboard, adding extra boxes as needed. That organizer served as a master plan for achieving the class's goal.

Intermediate Grades

Fourth graders studying the middle ages used the graphic organizer to record their impressions of feudal hierarchy.

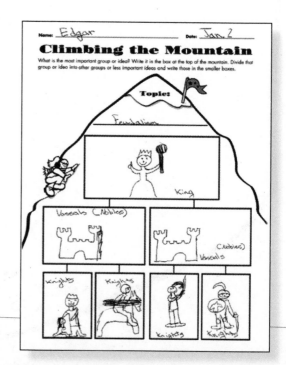

Climbing the Mountain

What is the most important group or idea? Write it in the box at the top of the mountain. Divide that group or idea into other groups or less important ideas and write those in the smaller boxes.

Topic: _____

RIVER FLOW CHART

Purpose

Flow charts help students to arrange events or the steps of a process in a logical order. The River Flow Chart can be used to describe the stages of an event, the actions of a character, or the steps in a procedure. Sequencing helps students recall key events and understand how events are related to each other.

How to Use the Organizer

Students can work alone or in small groups to list the events they need to sequence. If students have difficulty ordering the events chronologically, guide their thinking by asking questions such as, "What was the first thing that happened? What happened next?" Younger students may find it easier to record the beginning and the end, and then fill in important events that took place in between. You may also want to suggest that students work backwards, starting with the final outcome, and recording the events that led to the outcome. This is a particularly good strategy for recognizing causal relationships within a series of events. Students need not use all of the stepping stones on the organizer. If necessary, they may also draw and number extra stones on the back of their papers for additional steps or events.

Skills

Students will:

+ **recall key events**

+ **identify steps in a process**

+ **sequence events in a logical order**

+ **recognize causal relationships**

Examples

Primary Grades

Third graders used the organizer to take notes while watching a video on the history of money. Students were asked to record the events chronologically. The amount of detail that students included on their organizers gave the teacher a means for assessing their ability to sequence events and their understanding of the material.

Intermediate Grades

At the end of a unit on the U.S. Congress, a fifth-grade teacher gave his students a random list of the basic steps for passing a law and asked the students to put the steps in order. The organizer enabled both the students and their teacher to assess at a glance his students' understanding of the process.

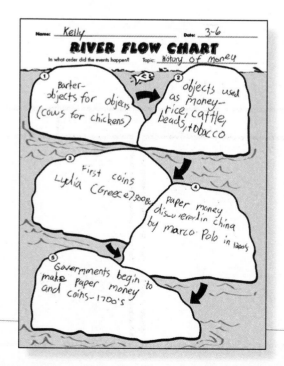

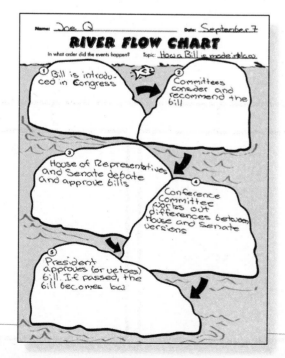

RIVER FLOW CHART

In what order did the events happen?   Topic: _____

1

2

3

4

5

CAUSE-AND-EFFECTS TREE

✦✦ Skills

Students will:

✦ **identify causes and effects**

✦ **recognize that a cause can have multiple effects**

✦ **investigate causal relationships**

Purpose

Identifying causes and effects helps students understand the consequences of actions and events both throughout history and in their own lives. Understanding causal relationships is an important critical thinking skill that leads to a deeper understanding of subject matter and allows students to make connections between their learning and their own lives. Students who can recognize the results of actions or events are better able to make choices about their own behavior.

How to Use the Organizer

Be sure that students understand that a cause is an action or event that makes something else (the effect) happen. If necessary, review simple cause-and-effect relationships such as "If I knock that glass over (cause), the water will spill (effect)." Have students identify a cause and write it on the tree trunk. If all students are exploring the effects of the same cause, write the cause on the tree trunk before making copies of the organizer. Students can work together or individually to identify and record the effects on the branches of the tree. To show multiple causes for one effect (for example, the causes of the Civil War), change the labels on the organizer before making copies for the class. Write EFFECT on the tree trunk and CAUSE on each of the branches.

Examples

Primary Grades

When a class of second graders complained about new lunchroom rules, their teacher used the issue to illustrate the connection between student behavior and school rules. He asked students to make a list of the new rules. While viewing the organizer on the interactive whiteboard, he recorded each rule on a branch of the tree.

Intermediate Grades

Cooperative groups of sixth graders were asked to research a historical movement and report on its short- and long-term effects. Students first recorded their ideas on individual organizers. After discussing the ideas, each group selected what they felt were the most important effects of the historical movement and recorded the results on large construction-paper Cause and Effects Trees, which they contributed to a classroom bulletin board.

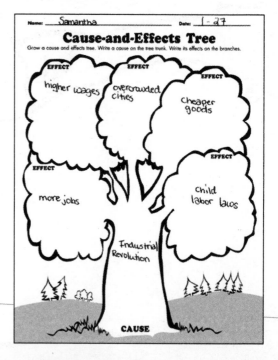

Cause-and-Effects Tree

Grow a cause-and-effects tree. Write a cause on the tree trunk. Write its effects on the branches.

EFFECT

EFFECT

EFFECT

EFFECT

EFFECT

CAUSE

HEAR YE! HEAR YE!

Skills

Students will:

+ relate prior knowledge to new concepts

+ summarize key concepts

+ record new content knowledge

+ identify key vocabulary

Purpose

Students who respond personally to what they read or hear in class are engaged, thoughtful learners. The NICK list gives students a way to structure their responses: first by taking notes on the new information being presented, then by recording prior knowledge and impressions sparked by the information, and lastly by focusing on key vocabulary words and their meanings. Because the organizer helps students process complex information, it works well both as a prewriting tool and as a study guide for tests.

How to Use the Organizer

To introduce the organizer, draw three columns on the chalkboard and label them with the headings shown on the organizer. Read aloud a brief passage containing factual material. Slowly reread the passage, pausing to record notes about your reading in the first column on the chalkboard. In the second column, record questions that might pop up or information you might recall while you are reading. When you have finished rereading the selection, ask students to help you identify key vocabulary from the passage. Record the words and their meanings in the third column. (You may need to reread sections of the passage so that students can use context clues to determine the meaning of the words.)

Examples

Primary Grades

A small group of third graders read "A Woman Called Moses," an article in their weekly news supplement, and used the organizer to record their impressions of the information presented in the article. The teacher used the organizer to assess the students' comprehension of the article.

Intermediate Grades

A sixth-grade teacher encouraged her students to use the organizer for note-taking as they read assigned sections of their Social Studies textbook. During class discussion, students shared the comments they had recorded in the "Information & Comments" column and discussed any questions that had not been answered in their reading. Students used the organizers as study guides for weekly quizzes and unit tests.

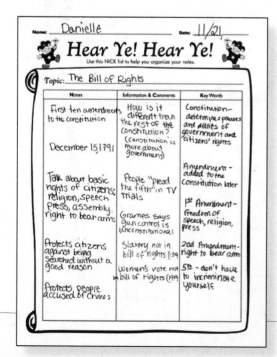

Name: _____   **Date:** _____

Hear Ye! Hear Ye!

Use this NICK list to help you organize your notes.

Topic:_____

Notes	**I**nformation & **C**omments	**K**ey Words

ORGANIZING POWER

 Skills

Students will:

+ **collect and categorize information**

+ **identify characteristics of people, places, or events**

+ **recognize relationships between facts**

Purpose

Recording information according to classifications or categories gives students the opportunity to organize and analyze the information in a variety of different ways. Students are able to see how facts within categories relate to each other and how the categories themselves relate to the topic as a whole. Students who are able to identify key features of a person, place, or event are more likely to understand how the features work together to form the unique character of the topic as a whole.

How to Use the Organizer

On the chalkboard, draw a circle with spokes branching off of it. Write the topic in the circle, and ask students to help you brainstorm categories to write on each spoke. Next, draw two or three lines off of each spoke. The diagram should now look like the Organizing Power organizer without the windmill illustration. Ask volunteers to suggest details to write on the lines under each category. Remind students that they can use the organizer to research and organize information for their own writing or to identify main ideas and details in material that they read.

Examples

Primary Grades

At the end of a unit on Africa, a third-grade teacher asked her students to complete the Organizing Power organizer with information about the continent. The class brainstormed a list of categories, which the teacher wrote on the chalkboard. Each student chose categories from the list and completed the organizer by filling in details for each category.

Intermediate Grades

As a culminating project on ancient civilizations, pairs of sixth-grade students created civilizations of their own. Students first determined major elements of culture, such as religion, government, or social organization. As they developed their civilizations, they recorded details about each element on the organizer. Finally, each pair of students used the information they had recorded to write an encyclopedia entry on their new civilization.

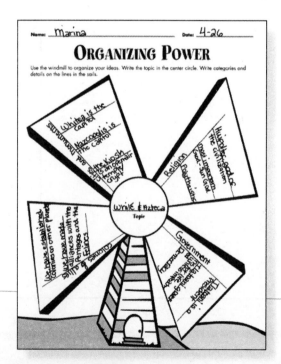

ORGANIZING POWER

Use the windmill to organize your ideas. Write the topic in the center circle. Write categories and details on the lines in the sails.

Topic

SHOOT FOR THE CIRCLES

Skills

Students will:

+ **compare and contrast times, places, economic systems, or cultures**

+ **identify distinguishing characteristics**

+ **record similarities and differences**

Purpose

Venn diagrams can be used with students to compare and contrast two items. Shoot for the Circles gives students a means for identifying key characteristics and recording similarities and differences. This graphic organizer requires students to recognize interrelationships and commonalities—a critical thinking skill that is fundamental to all social studies.

How to Use the Organizer

Students can use the organizer when comparing or contrasting two ideas or topics. Have students choose two topics that they wish to compare. Next, suggest that they brainstorm lists of distinguishing characteristics for each topic. As they record the characteristics on the organizer, remind them to write similarities in the overlapping section of the two circles. Information that is unique to one topic or the other goes in the non-intersecting parts of the circle.

For younger students, you may wish to introduce the organizer by making a "real" Venn diagram out of two circles of string. Label one circle "Shoes That Tie" and another circle "White Shoes." Ask each student to place his or her shoe in the appropriate section of the diagram.

Examples

Primary Grades

During a discussion of school safety rules, a first-grade teacher asked her students to brainstorm a list of safety rules that they had in their homes. The teacher used the information they provided to complete the Shoot for the Circles organizer on the interactive whiteboard so that students could see the overlap between rules they encounter at home and at school.

Intermediate Grades

Pairs of sixth graders were assigned the task of comparing two groups of indigenous peoples. These students chose to compare two Native American tribes. The students took notes as they researched individual tribes on the Internet. They recorded their information on the organizer, which the teacher used to assess their research.

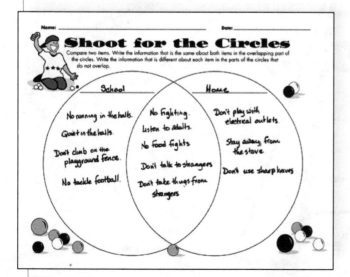

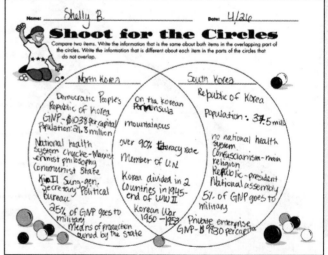

Shoot for the Circles

Compare two items. Write the information that is the same about both items in the overlapping part of the circles. Write the information that is different about each item in the parts of the circles that do not overlap.

MATRIX

✦ Skills

Students will:

+ **identify variables that lead to classification**

+ **compare and contrast objects according to variables**

+ **recognize patterns and relationships**

Purpose

The Matrix helps students to recognize that scientists use common attributes to classify objects in our environment. In coming up with a list of variables, students tap their prior knowledge and question their assumptions (and sometimes their misconceptions). As they compare and contrast objects, patterns emerge. These patterns help students to raise new questions and continue to expand their knowledge of the subject.

How to Use the Organizer

Begin by raising a question: "What is a simple machine?" "What conducts electricity?" Write this question in the left-hand corner of the matrix. Next, have students suggest the variables that define a category. For instance, one variable for a simple machine is that it produces force. List those variables across the top of the matrix. (If students disagree on a variable, suggest that they do some research—the variable can be added to the matrix later if necessary.) Then have students list objects that may or may not belong to the classification down the side of the matrix. Encourage students to suggest objects that are difficult to classify. Have students complete the matrix by placing pluses or minuses next to each word under each attribute. Follow this activity with a group discussion of patterns and conclusions.

Examples

Primary Grades

To introduce the topic of living organisms, a first-grade teacher projected the Matrix organizer on the interactive whiteboard. Together, the class generated criteria that distinguished living from nonliving things. Then the children brainstormed a list of objects in their environment and told whether they met each of the requirements of a living organism.

Intermediate Grades

After making a list of animals, fourth graders used specific criteria to determine which animals would be classified as mammals. By using the Matrix, children discovered that certain groups of animals share criteria (for instance mammals and birds are both warm-blooded) but that in order to be classified in one group, an animal must meet *all* of the criteria.

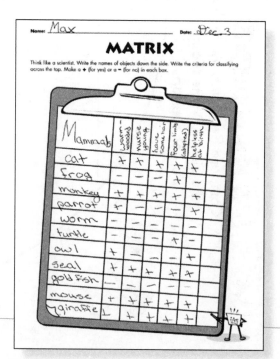

MATRIX

Think like a scientist. Write the names of objects down the side. Write the criteria for classifying across the top. Make a **+** (for yes) or a **−** (for no) in each box.

SORT AND CLASSIFY

Skills

Students will:

+ **select attributes for sorting**

+ **observe differences and similarities among objects or events**

+ **draw conclusions based on categorizations**

Purpose

Learning to observe differences in physical properties, and to classify objects or events according to attributes and properties, is the basis for scientific investigation. This organizer helps students make decisions regarding classification and to visualize the data that they've collected and sorted.

How to Use the Organizer

Whenever possible, provide children with actual objects to investigate. Ask them to observe the objects and come up with three sorting rules. Have them write the sorting rules on the lines within the leaves. (You can provide the sorting rules if you want students to pay close attention to specific attributes.) As students determine how they want to classify objects, have them draw a picture or write the name in the proper leaf. Suggest students work in small groups to discuss placement decisions, which will lead to greater understanding of classification. This organizer can also be used to record the results of experiments. For instance, after tasting different foods, children can record their names under the sorting rules of salty, sweet, or sour.

Examples

Primary Grades

At the end of a unit on plants and their uses, second-grade students demonstrated what they had learned by classifying plants used for food. Some of the students chose to include this organizer in their portfolio.

Intermediate Grades

In small groups, fourth-grade students classified ways of helping to preserve the environment. After generating ideas in small groups, they came together to discuss ways to reduce, reuse, and recycle in their own classroom.

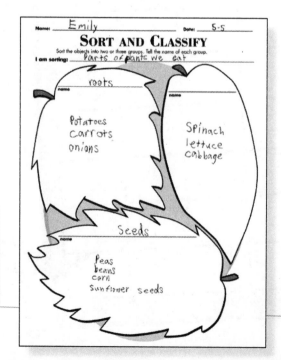

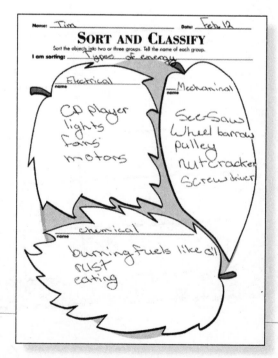

SORT AND CLASSIFY
Sort the objects into two or three groups. Tell the name of each group.

I am sorting: _____

name _____

name _____

name _____

OBSERVATION DIARY

Skills

Students will:

+ record observations

+ describe natural changes

+ identify causes and effects

+ draw conclusions based on observations

Purpose

In order for children to truly understand the nature of biology, physical science, or chemistry, they need to develop their powers of observation. As they view changes, they will begin to develop hypotheses concerning the causes and effects, and later develop experiments to test their hypotheses. This organizer gives students practice in recording and sharing observations.

How to Use the Organizer

Introduce the Observation Diary organizer by asking students to consider the job of a scientist. Make a list of the behaviors scientists must practice to be good at what they do. Guide students to understand that scientists must be careful observers, they must record small details that may be of great importance, and that they need to speculate why changes in what they are observing occur. Next, ask students to independently observe changes in something the class is studying over time. Later, bring students together to share their observations and discuss their hypothesis as to why the changes happened.

Examples

Primary Grades

A first-grade student observed her jack-o-lantern decomposing on the windowsill. While sharing her Observation Diary, she suggested that the black specks were living organisms. The first-grade teacher agreed to bring in a microscope so the children could test this hypothesis before the pumpkin was discarded.

Intermediate Grades

A fifth grader chose to begin an ant farm for his science fair project. After observing the farm for three weeks, he posted his Observation Diary pages for other students to read. Research notes on how ants work together and how they bury their dead accompanied the observations.

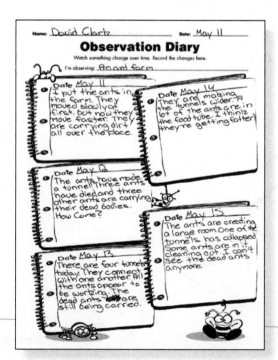

Name: cassiDy   Date: 6/2

Observation Diary

Watch something change over time. Record the changes here.

I'm observing: our Jack-o-lahtern

Date Nov 2
His eyes and nose are drooping He's wrinkly.

Date Nov 3
He looks squished He has fuzz growing inside.

Date Nov 4
There's lots more fuzz He is a little smelly.

Date Nov 6
He's very squishy Mr clark says we have to throw him out today. He smells!

Date Nov 5
There are black specks on the fuzz. They are alive He has a puddle of goo around him

Name: David Clark   Date: May 11

Observation Diary

Watch something change over time. Record the changes here.

I'm observing: An ant farm

Date May 11
I put the ants in the farm. They moved slowly at first, but now they move faster. They are carrying dirt all over the place.

Date May 14
They are making the tunnels wider. A lot of the ants are in the food tube. I think they're getting fatter!

Date May 12
The ants have made a tunnel. Three ants have died, and three other ants are carrying their dead bodies. How come?

Date May 15
The ants are creating a large room. One of the tunnels has collapsed. Some ants are in it cleaning out. I can't see the dead ants anymore.

Date May 13
There are four tunnels today. They connect with one another. All the ants appear to be working. The dead ants are still being carried.

58

Observation Diary

Watch something change over time. Record the changes here.

I'm observing: _____

Date: _____

Date: _____

Date: _____

Date: _____

Date: _____

FOCUS ON A CYCLE

✦ Skills

Students will:

✦ **observe and record natural cycles**

✦ **record events in sequential order**

✦ **demonstrate knowledge of stages**

Purpose

The Focus on a Cycle graphic organizer helps children to recall, organize, and visualize the sequential steps to a process. They come to realize that not all processes have a beginning, middle, and end, but are continual.

How to Use the Organizer

Introduce this organizer by asking children to consider a well-known cycle, such as the pattern of a typical school day. (If you use the school day, ask for general events such as arriving at school, working in the classroom, lunch, recess—so as not to invite discussion concerning minor variations.) As children tell you the major events in order, draw picture representations clockwise around the interior edge of the magnifying glass. Help them to draw the conclusion that Monday through Friday, they take part in a cycle. Next, ask children to consider the cycle they are currently studying in science and to depict it on this organizer. Once children are familiar with the organizer, you might suggest that they observe cycles in nature and record their findings on the organizer. Focus on a Cycle also lends itself to determining students' misconceptions about scientific cycles. Have children fill one out at the beginning of a unit of study to discover what they do know, and then again at the end of the unit to measure what they have learned.

Examples

Primary Grades

A third grader observed the life cycle of a butterfly and recorded her findings on the Focus on a Cycle graphic organizer.

Intermediate Grades

Small groups of fifth graders were asked to observe and keep a monthly journal of the moon's activity. When the month had passed, students compared their findings and presented their new knowledge on this organizer.

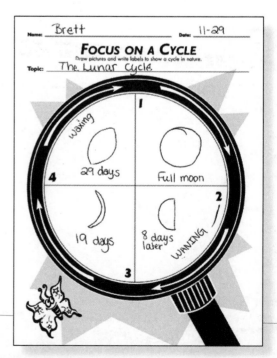

Name: _____   **Date:** _____

FOCUS ON A CYCLE
Draw pictures and write labels to show a cycle in nature.

Topic: _____

1

2

3

4

WEATHER WATCHER

✦✦ Skills

Students will:

✦ observe weather changes

✦ plot changing temperatures on a line graph

✦ make connections between weather and temperature patterns

Purpose

By observing and recording weather and temperature patterns, students can begin to hypothesize and question connections. Is the temperature always below 32 degrees Fahrenheit when it snows? If a weather pattern remains the same, does the temperature remain the same, too? By testing hypotheses students will begin to understand cause and effect relationships—the basis of weather forecasting.

How to Use the Organizer

Show students how to record the daily weather with the use of weather symbols like those in the corner. If students wish to be even more specific—for instance, if they wish to represent wind or sleet—encourage them to design their own symbols. Next, have them use a thermometer to record the outside temperature and record their findings with a dot on the graph below. If necessary, show them how to draw lines between the dots to create a line graph. Ask questions to lead students to new insights about weather changes and temperature. Whenever possible, have children generate hypotheses to test for further insight. (For children who are ready to compare weather patterns and temperature, make sure that someone continues to take data over the weekends.)

Examples

Primary Grades

After a first-grade class had recorded the data on the Weather Watcher during morning meeting for two weeks, the teacher explored common misperceptions. Her questions included, "Is it always warmest on sunny days?" and "Does rain always follow cloudy days?"

Intermediate Grades

For science homework, fourth-grade students were asked to record weather data twice a day for two weeks. Small groups came up with a hypothesis regarding temperature and weather patterns and devised ways to test their hypothesis. In addition, the class was invited to predict the next day's weather for a week. The predictions and the actual results were recorded on separate organizers and compared.

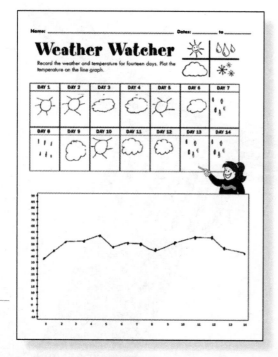

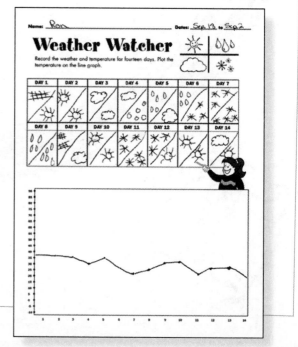

Weather Watcher

Record the weather and temperature for fourteen days. Plot the temperature on the line graph.

DAY 1	DAY 2	DAY 3	DAY 4	DAY 5	DAY 6	DAY 7

DAY 8	DAY 9	DAY 10	DAY 11	DAY 12	DAY 13	DAY 14

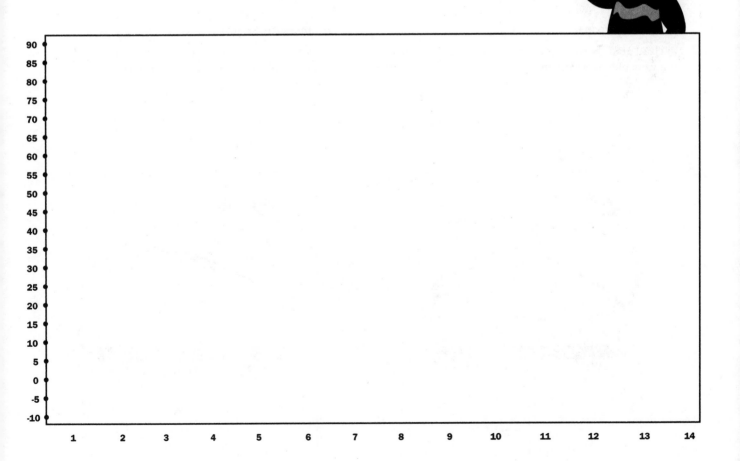

INVENTING INVENTIONS

✦ Skills

Students will:

✦ **identify cause and effect relationships**

✦ **analyze the effectiveness of inventions**

✦ **synthesize information to imagine or create their own inventions**

Purpose

The Inventing Inventions graphic organizer helps students to recognize that getting an original idea is just the first step of the inventor's process. Ideas must be combined with scientific knowledge, creativity, and plenty of trial and error before something new is created. Students come to recognize that the more knowledge we gain in the sciences, the more possibility there is for invention.

How to Use the Organizer

Model the use of this organizer by choosing a well-known invention. Record the necessity for the invention in the top space. Write the procedure that the inventor followed in the second space. You may want to point out that all inventors use the knowledge that has been acquired by other scientists. Although we credit one inventor, the process of invention is collaborative. Then show students how to follow the flow chart to record whether or not the attempt was successful. Students can use this graphic organizer to chart their own inventive processes as well.

Examples

Primary Grades

Third graders were asked to research the history of a valuable invention and to share their findings with the class.

Intermediate Grades

Fifth-grade students were challenged to create their own inventions. Inventions were presented at a science fair.

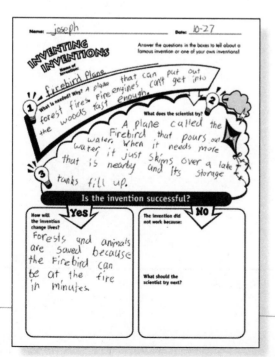

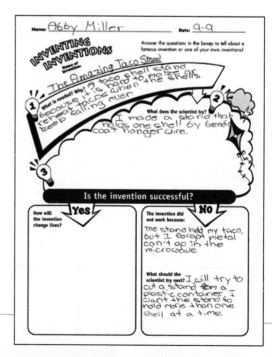

Name: _____ Date: _____

INVENTING INVENTIONS

Answer the questions in the boxes to tell about a famous invention or one of your own inventions!

Name of Invention: _____

1 What is needed? Why?

2 What does the scientist try?

3

Is the invention successful?

Yes

How will the invention change lives?

No

The invention did not work because:

What should the scientist try next?

THE SCIENTIFIC METHOD

Skills

Students will:

+ **identify steps of the scientific method**

+ **record from experimentation**

+ **draw conclusions based on evidence**

Purpose

The graphic organizer guides students through the five steps of the scientific method. It gives them a structure for exploring scientific questions and helps them to present the results of experiments, in addition to their reasons for drawing particular conclusions, to others.

How to Use the Organizer

Explain to students that the scientific method is a set of general rules that scientists have used for hundreds of years. By presenting information in a systematic way, scientists can follow and replicate another scientist's process. Introduce this organizer to the class by raising a question about the topic you are studying. Have students record the question in the first beaker. Ask students to predict the answer to the question and write their prediction in the second beaker. Explain that the prediction is called a *hypothesis*. Next, guide students to record the steps of an experiment. You might want to suggest that they number the steps. Then encourage students to conduct the experiment and record the data in the fourth beaker. Finally, ask them to draw conclusions by interpreting the data they collected. Are they surprised by the conclusion?

Examples

Primary Grades

A second-grade teacher completed the first and third beaker before photocopying this graphic organizer for her students. She placed the organizer in the science learning center, where students recorded their hypotheses, data, and conclusions while conducting the experiment on the weight of liquids.

Intermediate Grades

A sixth-grade student chose to conduct an experiment on mold and completed this organizer at home for extra credit in science. Her teacher keeps this option open to students throughout the school year.

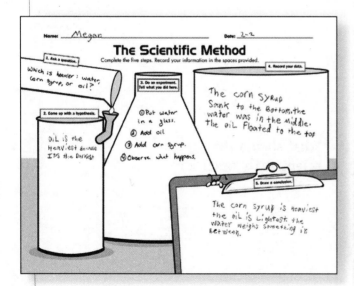

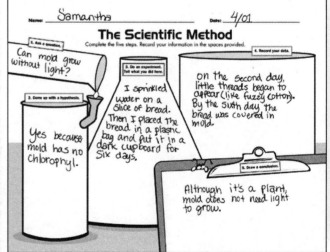

The Scientific Method

Complete the five steps. Record your information in the spaces provided.

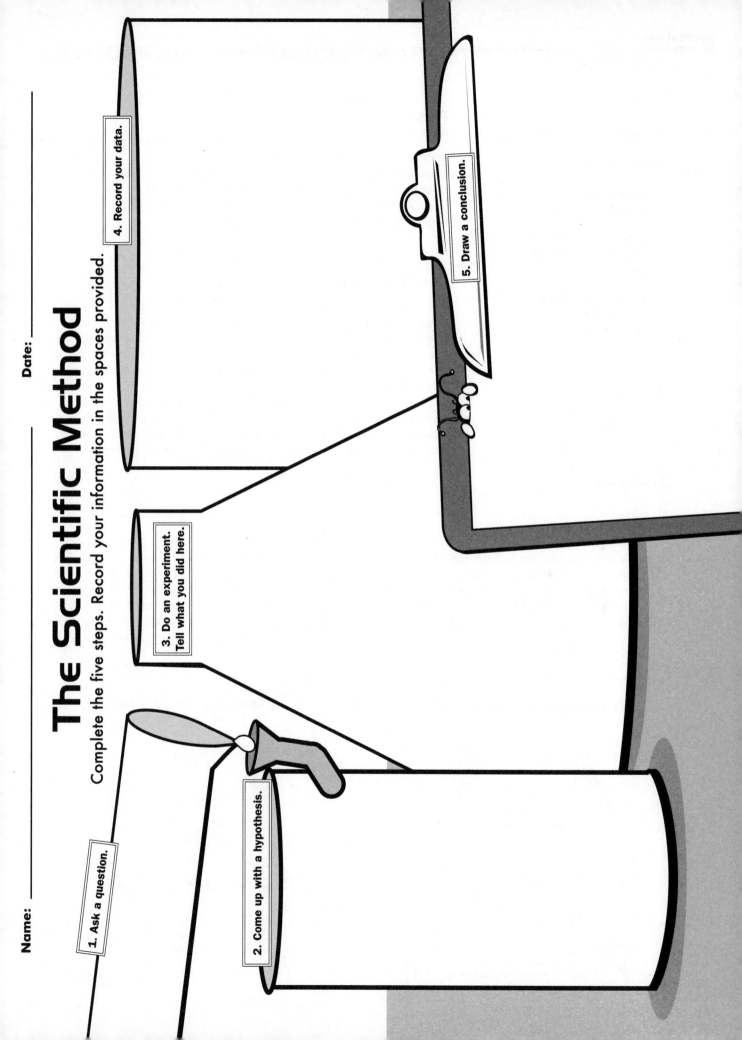

1. Ask a question.

2. Come up with a hypothesis.

3. Do an experiment. Tell what you did here.

4. Record your data.

5. Draw a conclusion.

★ PLAN YOUR SCIENCE FAIR PROJECT

Purpose

One of the most difficult tasks of designing and presenting a science fair project is determining a suitable topic. The Plan Your Science Fair Project organizer helps students to think about a particular choice: *Do I have resources? Can I gather the necessary materials? How will I demonstrate knowledge?* Preplanning will help students evaluate the suitability of their topic and help them to budget their time.

How to Use the Organizer

After you have presented your criteria for science fair projects, invite students to use this organizer to help them explore their ideas. Suggest that they brainstorm a list of topics and record them in the top car. Point out that the most successful projects are those that genuinely interest the scientist and that can be managed within the time period. Once they have decided on a topic, have them write it in the center of the organizer. Allow them to do research to complete the rest of the graphic organizer. If a student has difficulty coming up with resources or materials, or if the topic does not lend itself to a demonstration, suggest that the student explore one of the other topics by completing a new organizer.

Examples

Primary Grades

A third-grade student chose to study the body's reaction time, since her softball coach had just discussed this topic. She did some preliminary research and made up her own experiment as a homework assignment.

Intermediate Grades

In a science fair competition, a team of sixth graders chose to study the factors that affect electricity. This graphic shows their second attempt to find a suitable topic. Their first attempt, to determine the effect of water on paper towels, proved to be too simple when compared to the projects of classmates.

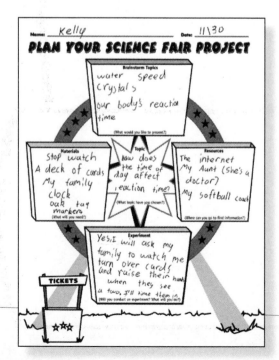

Name: _____   Date: _____

PLAN YOUR SCIENCE FAIR PROJECT

Brainstorm Topics

(What would you like to present?)

Materials

(What will you need?)

Topic

(What topic have you chosen?)

Resources

(Where can you go to find information?)

Experiment

(Will you conduct an experiment? What will you do?)

TICKETS

★ ★ ★

COMPARE AND CONTRAST

✦ Skills

Students will:

+ **identify prior knowledge of the topic**

+ **research and record important ideas**

+ **compare and contrast facts to see relationships**

Purpose

The Venn diagram, or in this case Venn bubbles, helps students to visualize important relationships between similar objects or events. Students can use this graphic to organize and show what they know about a topic (at the beginning or end of a unit), make connections as they read and do research, or to record information gleaned from investigations.

How to Use the Organizer

Model the use of this organizer by comparing and contrasting objects or events with multiple attributes. For instance, you might compare three different lunches that students have brought to school, or the way in which three different subjects are taught in your classroom. Have students record the names of objects or events on the lines inside the bubbles. Then have students call out attributes. If two or more objects have the same attributes, show students how to record the information in the place where the appropriate circles overlap. If all three objects or events share the same attributes, demonstrate recording information in the center where all three circles overlap. Comparing and contrasting three elements requires advanced organizational skills. You may want to begin by using graphic organizers that compare and contrast two elements first (pages 20 and 52).

Examples

Primary Grades

A third-grade student used this graphic organizer to organize what she was learning about clouds. She completed one draft and then copied the information onto a second organizer (shown here). Students often find that the placement of the information in the graphic organizer changes as they learn more.

Intermediate Grades

A sixth-grade teacher suggested that students complete a Compare and Contrast organizer to include in their reports about the earth. Making comparisons helped students to understand that water, temperature, and the earth's atmosphere allow it to support life in the universe.

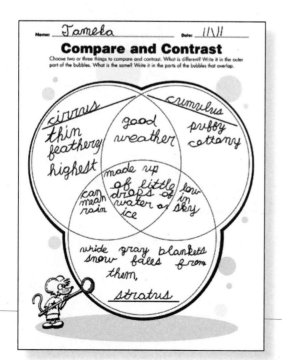

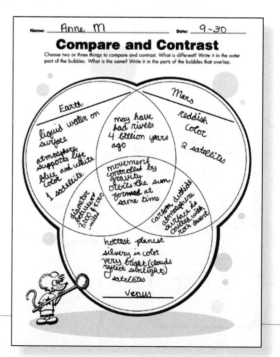

Compare and Contrast

Choose two or three things to compare and contrast. What is different? Write it in the outer part of the bubbles. What is the same? Write it in the parts of the bubbles that overlap.

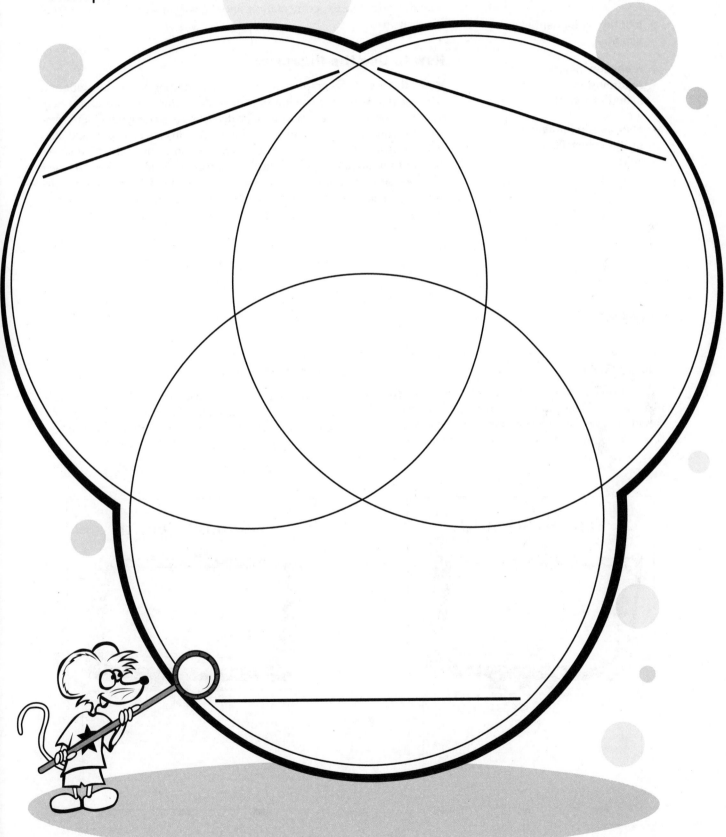

FAMOUS SCIENTIST

✦ Skills

Students will:

✦ **identify an influential scientist**

✦ **recall key points regarding the scientist's work**

✦ **analyze the influence of the scientific work**

Purpose

By taking a close look at one scientist and the work that he or she has done, students begin to see the cause and effect relationship between a scientific vocation, experimentation, and the way in which science affects our daily lives.

How to Use the Organizer

Model the use of this graphic organizer by illustrating and writing about a scientist that you have studied or will study in the near future. You may want to show children how you make decisions regarding which information to choose by "thinking out loud." For instance, you might say, "I know that Louis Pasteur was the son of a tanner, but this information does not tell me about his scientific discoveries or how he has changed our lives, so I will not include it." After you have modeled the use of this organizer, students can complete their own individually or in small groups.

Examples

Primary Grades

A second-grade student completed the graphic organizer after reading about Dian Fossey in her student weekly newspaper. The organizer was posted on a school bulletin board about famous scientists.

Intermediate Grades

One fifth-grade teacher had students create a time line of famous scientists. This student's organizer represented a scientist from the early 17th century.

Famous Scientist

Draw or write about a famous scientist in the picture frame. Then write about his or her scientific discovery in the box below.

Scientist's
Name:

Tell about the scientist's discovery. How did it change lives?

GO FOR THE GOAL!

✦✦ Skills

Students will:

- ✦ demonstrate an under-standing of whole number operations

- ✦ develop proficiency with math facts

- ✦ use a variety of computation strategies to solve problems

Purpose

Learning basic math facts is one of the major stepping stones in elementary mathematics. Students who have a quick and accurate recall of basic math facts are better able to apply their computation skills to a wide range of problem-solving situations. Students can use the Go for the Goal! fact table to record what they know, test themselves on what they don't know, and gain practice and understanding through games and other interactive activities.

How to Use the Organizer

Depending upon the abilities of your students, you can use the fact table to chart either addition or multiplication facts. Before copying the organizer, write the appropriate symbols (+ or x) in the upper left corner of the chart. If necessary, display the organizer or draw a large copy on the chalkboard so that you can demonstrate how the grid works. Place one finger on a number in the first row, another on a number in the first column, and bring the two fingers together to meet at a square. Then perform the given operation and write the answer in the square.

Examples

Primary Grades

Pairs of second graders used the chart to practice basic addition facts in a game called Tic Tac Add. To play the game, students took turns rolling two dice, adding the numbers shown, and recording the answer in the appropriate squares on their Go for the Goal! sheets. The first player to fill in three squares in a row vertically, horizontally, or diagonally won the game.

Intermediate Grades

Fourth graders studying multiples used the organizer to create different designs. Students first filled in the squares so that each had a completed multiplication table. Next, each student chose a number between 2 and 12 and, using a colored pencil colored in each square where a multiple of that number appeared on the chart. Students compared their designs and, as an extension, colored in a second set of multiples in a different color to create more elaborate, multi-colored patterns.

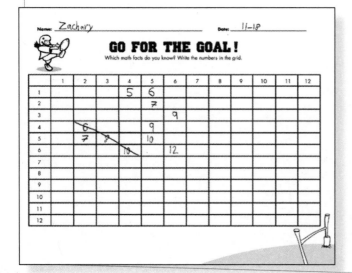

GO FOR THE GOAL!

Which math facts do you know? Write the numbers in the grid.

	1	2	3	4	5	6	7	8	9	10	11	12
1												
2												
3												
4												
5												
6												
7												
8												
9												
10												
11												
12												

PUZZLE PIECES

✦✧ Skills

Students will:

✦ **model numeric relationships**

✦ **use basic operations to solve problems**

✦ **determine the number in a set by combining, separating, or rearranging its parts**

Purpose

Much of the computation work done in the elementary grades centers on combining or separating sets—addition or subtraction. However, simply knowing how to add or subtract does not guarantee that a student will know how to apply those skills in problem-solving situations. Part-Part-Whole diagrams like the Puzzle Pieces organizer give students a way to represent changes in quantity, combinations, missing parts, and comparisons.

How to Use the Organizer

To introduce the organizer, cut a large sheet of construction paper into three puzzle pieces representing the pieces of the organizer. Label the pieces "PART," "PART," and "WHOLE" and demonstrate how the pieces fit together. Write a sample problem on the chalkboard. Read through the problem. Then return to key numbers and ask, "In this problem, is this a part or a whole?" Write the numbers on the appropriate pieces of the puzzle and ask a volunteer to solve the problem to find the missing piece.

Examples

Primary Grades

Pairs of first graders were given ten pencils and asked to find a solution to the following problem:

Divide ten pencils into two groups. One group should have two more pencils than the other group does. How many are in each group?

The students experimented with different combinations and recorded their findings by drawing ten pencils in the WHOLE box and then drawing smaller groups of pencils in the PART boxes.

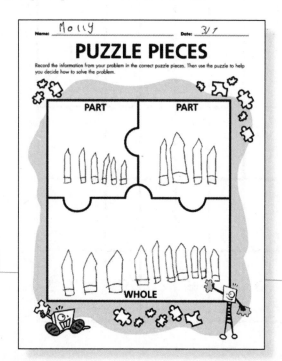

Intermediate Grades

A fifth grader struggling with missing addend problems used the organizer to help her decide which operation to use to solve the following problem:

There are 526 children in our school. 268 of them are boys. How many girls are there?

Seeing the numbers in their proper places on the diagram reminded the student that she needed to use subtraction, not addition, to find the unknown part.

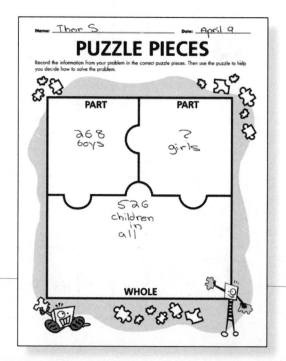

PUZZLE PIECES

Record the information from your problem in the correct puzzle pieces. Then use the puzzle to help you decide how to solve the problem.

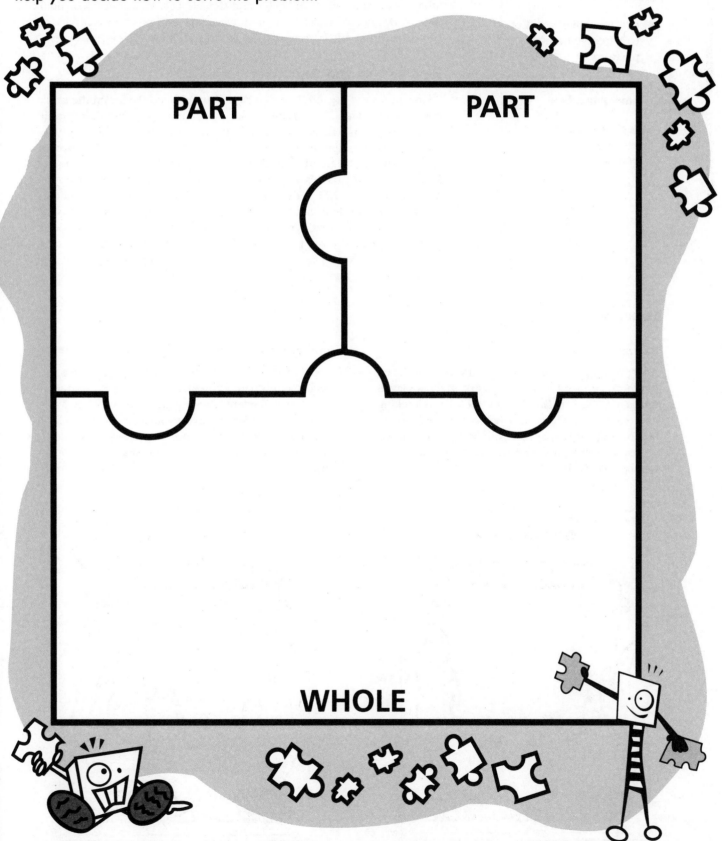

PART

PART

WHOLE

NUMBER SOUP

Students will:

+ **use reasoning abilities to perceive number patterns**

+ **identify relationships among numbers**

+ **test and justify reasonability of conclusions**

Purpose

Number sense—the sense of how numbers are related to each other and how they work—is the foundation of all mathematical knowledge. Students need a solid knowledge and flexible curiosity about how numbers work to make sense of the computational methods they learn and to be able to apply those computation skills to problem-solving situations.

How to Use the Organizer

To introduce the organizer, draw a large soup pot and flames on the chalkboard. Tell students, "I'm going to make a number soup, but only certain ingredients go into my soup. Can you suggest some ingredients?" Think of a "rule," such as a number or number relationship. Write a few numbers or expressions that fit the rule inside the pot, and a few numbers that do not fit the rule in the flames. For example, for the rule "divisible by five," you might write *5, 25, 125* in the pot and *2, 24, 99* in the flames. Tell students that you have a rule in mind, and that any numbers or expressions that fit that rule can go into the pot. As students suggest numbers or expressions, write them either in the pot (if they fit the rule) or in the flames (if they don't). After each suggestion, pause and ask, "Do you know what the rule is for this number soup?"

Examples

Primary Grades

After using manipulatives to explore odd and even numbers, cooperative groups of first graders played the game "Odd or Even." They took turns picking random numbers out of a hat and recording the numbers in the proper place on the graphic organizer—even numbers inside the soup pot, and odd numbers in the fire.

Intermediate Grades

Sixth graders used the Number Soup organizer to record equivalent expressions for a variety of numbers. Each student chose a different number and wrote ten equivalent expressions or "names" for the number in the soup pot. Expressions included the results of operations, exponential expressions, arrays, and drawings.

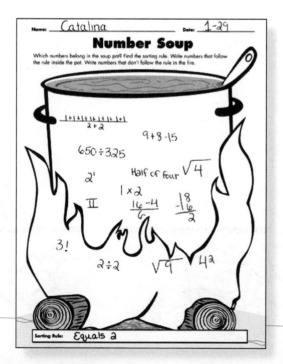

Number Soup

Which numbers belong in the soup pot? Find the sorting rule. Write numbers that follow the rule inside the pot. Write numbers that don't follow the rule in the fire.

Sorting Rule: _____

MAKE A NUMBER

Purpose

A strong understanding of place value is critical to a student's proficiency in computational skills. In order to perform even basic operations such as addition and subtraction, students need to understand how the value of a digit changes depending upon its position in a number. They need to know how to read and write numbers, using zeros as place holders when necessary, and how to align sets of numbers so that the pencil-and-paper methods they learn for solving problems make sense. Writing numbers in place-value grids like the one on this organizer allows students to track digits visually and provides the support they need to perform computation operations with increased accuracy.

How to Use the Organizer

Project the Make A Number place value grid. Ask volunteers to call out large numbers. Write each number in the grid, noting the placement of each digit that you write. Then switch roles, and have volunteers write numbers that you suggest.

✦✦ Skills

Students will:

✦ **read and write numbers to the billions place**

✦ **represent place-value models as numerals**

✦ **develop proficiency in whole number operations**

Examples

Primary Grades

A second-grade teacher used the graphic organizer and base-ten blocks to reinforce place value concepts. Working with a small group, she used the blocks to "build" a number (for example, one hundred, two tens, and six ones). The students recorded the digits in the proper spaces on the chart. Then volunteers read each number aloud.

Intermediate Grades

A fourth-grade teacher found that although her students had good multiplication skills, their answers for double-digit multiplication problems were often inaccurate. She suggested that students use the organizer to help them keep the numbers in these complex problems aligned.

Make a Number

What numbers can you make? Use this grid to make new numbers.

billions	hundred millions	ten millions	millions	hundred thousands	ten thousands	thousands	hundreds	tens	ones

1 2 3 4 5 6 7 8 9 0

BALANCING ACT

Skills

Students will:

+ **identify and use equivalent forms of numbers, expressions, and measures**

+ **generate equivalencies**

+ **use words, drawings, and symbols to represent equivalencies and relationships**

Purpose

One of the underlying principles of mathematics is the understanding that a quantity may be expressed in a variety of different forms. From the time that kindergarteners first discover that one plus two equals three through the study of equivalent fractions, equal measures, and algebraic expressions, students work with concepts of equivalence. As students explore these concepts either with concrete objects or symbolically, they can use the organizer to record their observations.

How to Use the Organizer

Make a simple seesaw by balancing a ruler on the side of a pencil. Place a number of small objects or weights on either side of the ruler and ask, "Are these two sides equal? How can you tell?" Draw a seesaw on the chalkboard and record your findings on the drawing. Discuss with students strategies for finding equivalences in their current area of study and show students how to record the equivalences on the drawing.

Examples

Primary Grades

A group of second graders used Cuisenaire rods and balance scales to explore beginning multiplication concepts. The teacher gave each child a different number of red rods to place on one side of the scale and challenged the children to find out how many white rods they must place on the other side in order to make their scales balance. The students used colored pencils to record the results of their explorations on their graphic organizers.

Intermediate Grades

A measurement center in a fourth-grade classroom was set up with a tub of water and cup, pint, quart, and gallon containers. The teacher suggested that students use the materials to find equivalent measurements, such as how many cups are in a pint or a quart. Students recorded their findings by writing or drawing one measure on one side of the seesaw and an equivalent measure on the other side.

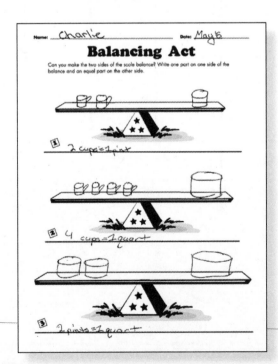

Balancing Act

Can you make the two sides of the scale balance? Write one part on one side of the balance and an equal part on the other side.

1

_____

2

_____

3

_____

PIECES OF THE PIE

Skills

Students will:

+ divide a circle into equal parts

+ organize information to put into a graph

+ use a circle graph to display data

+ interpret information on a graph

Purpose

Graphing helps students organize and display mathematical data in a visual manner. Circle graphs, or pie charts, represent data as parts of a whole. As younger students use the graphic organizer to represent fractional parts, they begin to understand the relationships between individual parts or "slices" and the whole. Older students will use the organizer to represent percentages, with the circle representing 100%.

How to Use the Organizer

To introduce the organizer, draw a large circle on the chalkboard. Divide the circle into fractional parts. (The level of difficulty will vary from class to class.) Draw and shade various parts of the whole as you review the names of the fractional parts. In the intermediate grades, refer to the graphic organizer and ask how many sections the circle is divided into (20), what part of the whole each section represents ($\frac{1}{20}$), and what percentage each section represents (5%). Collect some data about the class, such as the number of students who are wearing sneakers, and demonstrate how to represent the data as a fractional part of the circle.

Examples

Primary Grades

Third graders were asked to interview 20 classmates about their favorite colors and to organize their data according to the number of students who preferred each color. Using the marks on the Pieces of the Pie chart, the students divided their organizers into twenty sections and colored in one section for each student interviewed. As the students compared and discussed their graphs, their teacher used the opportunity to introduce the concept of equivalent fractions ($\frac{5}{20} = \frac{1}{4}$ of the circle).

Intermediate Grades

A sixth-grade class had been studying how to convert fractions into percentages. As part of an interdisciplinary research project, the students researched how land is used in different states. They each chose a state and recorded the amount of acreage used as cropland, forestland, pasture and rangeland, and developed land. The students then converted their findings into percentage of the state's total acreage and used the pie chart to display their results.

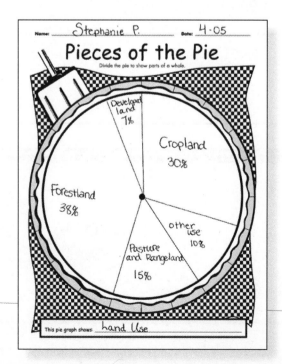

Pieces of the Pie

Divide the pie to show parts of a whole.

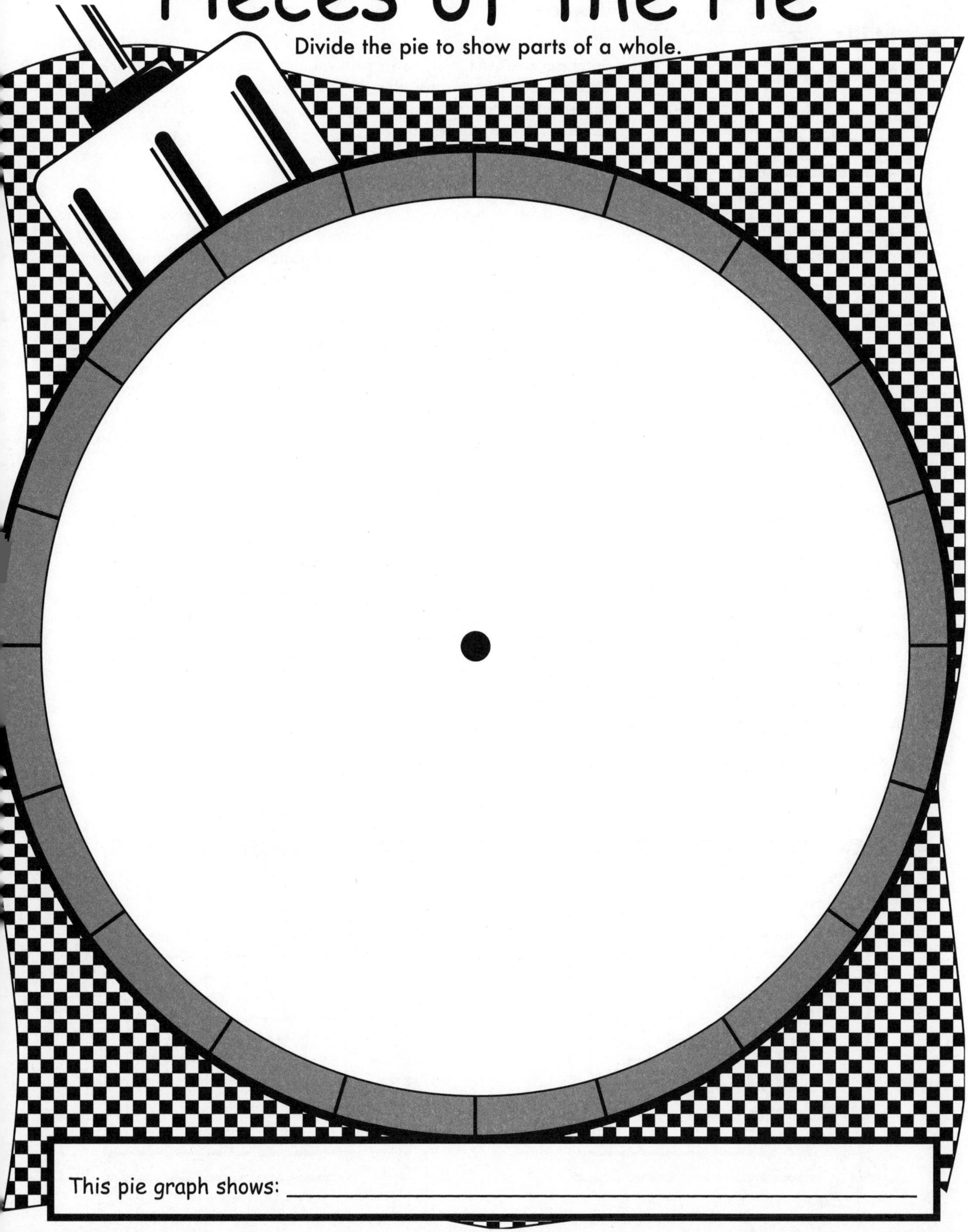

This pie graph shows: _____

GRAPH IT!

✦ Skills

Students will:

✦ collect and organize data

✦ draw conclusions from a set of data

✦ compare and contrast sets of data

Purpose

Graphing allows students to collect and organize data effectively, and to interpret that data to discover patterns, draw conclusions, and make predictions. Students can use this graphic organizer to organize and display statistical information in the form of bar graphs, picture graphs, line graphs, and coordinate graphs.

How to Use the Organizer

Ask students to help you gather information about the class, for example, types of shoes, hair color, or number of siblings. Then demonstrate how to organize and display the information on the Graph It! organizer. Write a title for the graph in the white space along the bottom edge, and fill in the shaded spaces along each axis with appropriate labels. Complete the graph, using the information you collected about the class. The type of graph you use will depend upon the kind of information you gather and how you want to interpret it. If the whole class is using the organizer to make the same type of graph, you may wish to fill in the labels before making copies for the students.

Examples

Primary Grades

Cooperative groups of first graders were given a bucket of plastic animals and asked to count how many of each type of animal were in the bucket. Their teacher labeled the organizer with simple drawings of the animals, and gave each group a copy of the graph. The groups then graphed their results, coloring in one square for each animal they had counted.

Intermediate Grades

A fourth grader kept track of her independent reading for one week. After collecting her data, she decided that a line graph would best show how her reading habits changed over the course of the week.

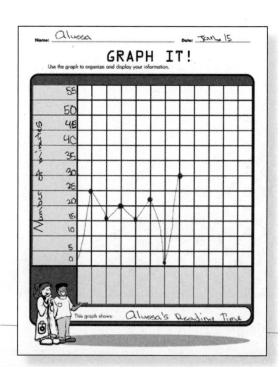

GRAPH IT!

Use the graph to organize and display your information.

This graph shows:

ROBOT RULES

Skills

Students will:

+ **recognize, describe, extend, and create numerical patterns**

+ **use patterns and relationships to solve problems**

+ **analyze relationships to show how a change affects quantities**

Purpose

Patterns are central to mathematical understanding. Recognizing and describing patterns is a powerful problem-solving tool that allows students to predict the results of changes in quantities. The Robot Rules organizer is set up to display ordered pairs of numbers. Younger students can use the organizer to record information about real-world patterns. Older students can use the organizer as a standard function table to solve algebraic problems.

How to Use the Organizer

To introduce the organizer, draw a large T-shaped function table on the chalkboard. Give students an example of a problem that can be solved by finding a pattern. For example, a primary-grade teacher might ask, "How many ears are in this room?" and have the class record the information in columns labeled "Number of People" and "Number of Ears." A teacher working with upper-grade students might write an equation such as $x + y = 10$ and record appropriate pairs of numbers in columns marked x and y. Suggest that students use the organizer to solve problems—by recording pairs of numbers, looking for patterns, and, if possible, finding a rule that will help them predict future results.

Examples

Primary Grades

Third graders used the graphic organizer to create price charts for the school store. Students looked for a pattern and, depending on their individual abilities, used addition or multiplication to complete the chart.

Name: Noah   Date: 9\8

ROBOT RULES

Fill in the spaces on the robot. Write the numbers that follow the rule.

RULE: Erasers—25¢ each

IN:	OUT:
1 eraser	$.25
2 erasers	$.50
3 erasers	$.75
4 erasers	$1.00
5 erasers	$1.25
6 erasers	$1.50
7 erasers	$1.75
8 erasers	$2.00

Intermediate Grades

Sixth graders in a pre-algebra class used the graphic organizer as a function table to solve the following problem:

Jessica has a dog-walking business. She charges $6.00 per hour of walking, plus an additional fee of $3.00 per dog. Last month, she spent 7 hours walking Fifi. How much should she charge Fifi's owners?

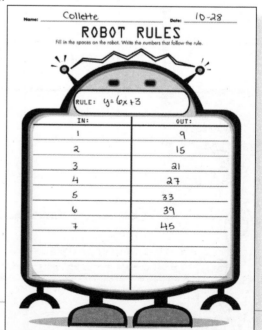

Name: Collette   Date: 10-28

ROBOT RULES

Fill in the spaces on the robot. Write the numbers that follow the rule.

RULE: $y = 6x + 3$

IN:	OUT:
1	9
2	15
3	21
4	27
5	33
6	39
7	45

ROBOT RULES

Fill in the spaces on the robot. Write the numbers that follow the rule.

RULE:

IN:	OUT:

STAR SOLVER

Skills

Students will:

+ **select appropriate problem-solving strategies**

+ **demonstrate solutions to mathematical problems**

+ **represent the process for solving mathematical problems**

Purpose

Mathematics, like science, has a universal problem-solving process. The Star Solver graphic organizer gives students a structure by which they can focus on the problem at hand, choose an appropriate problem-solving strategy, judge information as relevant or irrelevant, and demonstrate their ability to solve the problem.

How to Use the Organizer

To introduce the organizer, present the class with a problem, such as "Which of these containers can hold more beans?" (The level of difficulty will vary according to grade level.) Draw a large star on the chalkboard. Write or draw the problem in the top triangle. Then ask, "What information do we need to solve this problem?" Record the information in the far left triangle of the star. If there is extraneous information in the problem, record that in the far right triangle of the star. In the middle of the star, "arrange" the information so that students can see how to solve it. For example, in lower grades, you might want to draw pictures showing equalities or inequalities. Upper-grade students will probably write equations in this space.

Examples

Primary Grades

Second graders used the organizer to plan and record their methods of solving a capacity problem at a learning center. The center was set up with two large, empty containers; a cup measure; a dishpan full of beans; copies of the graphic organizer; and a card with the following problem printed on it: "Which container has the greater capacity?"

Intermediate Grades

Students in a fourth-grade class used the graphic organizer to help them solve word problems such as the following:

Alex will turn 18 in the year 2005. His sister will turn 15 in the same year. In what year was Alex born?

STAR SOLVER

Be a star problem solver. Write what you need to do in the spaces on the star.

What's the problem?

Information that's needed.

Arrange the information.

Information that's not needed.

Do the math.

Check the answer.

PUSH TOWARD LEARNING

✦✦ Skills

Students will:

+ **create a learning plan**

+ **keep records of their learning experiences**

+ **evaluate the results of their experience**

+ **set new goals**

Purpose

The five steps represented on the Push Toward Learning organizer encourage students to become more engaged in their own learning. The graphic organizer helps them to identify the purpose of activities, to brainstorm learning strategies, and to consider the criteria necessary for meeting learning goals. It also helps students to see learning and assessment as a continuous process by asking the question, "What next?"

How to Use the Organizer

You may want to have the class complete the organizer together several times before asking individuals to complete it on their own. After writing the topic of study in the center of the organizer, show students how to move from the lower left-hand boulder, up the hill, and then back down again. For the first boulder, suggest that children use questions to state what they need to learn, such as "How long is this room?" or "Who were the most influential leaders in the Civil War?" Next, suggest they come up with a variety of strategies for answering their questions. Students can design their own means of measuring the effectiveness of their strategies for the third boulder, or you can provide the criteria that you will be using to assess their projects. In boulder four, students reflect to assess their own learning. The answer to the question in the last boulder may relate to their project or state an entirely new learning goal.

Examples

Primary Grades

A second-grade teacher assisted a small group of students in planning a homework project on cultural diversity. The criteria for measuring the success of the learning were provided by the teacher.

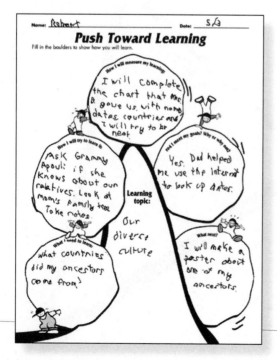

Intermediate Grades

Fifth graders planned long-range projects that showed how statistics affect their lives. This student chose to show the correlation between a television program's target audience and products advertised.

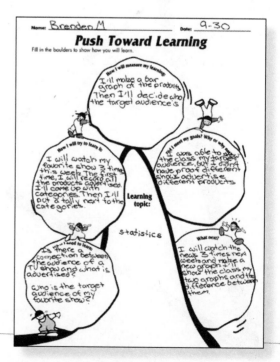

Push Toward Learning
Fill in the boulders to show how you will learn.

How I will measure my learning:

How I will try to learn it:

Did I meet my goals? Why or why not?

Learning topic:

What I need to learn:

What next?

STUDENT SELF-ASSESSMENT

✦✦ Skills

Students will:

✦ **evaluate their learning experiences**

✦ **initiate a plan for continuous learning**

Purpose

When students take an active part in the assessment process, they become more engaged learners. The Student Self-Assessment organizer encourages students to reflect on their learning and the success of the strategies they use. The organizer can be used to evaluate a student's involvement on a particular project, or to evaluate the student's progress over a learning period.

How to Use the Organizer

Introduce the organizer at the beginning of a project or a marking period to familiarize children with the process and the criteria they will be using to assess their progress. With students in grades one and two, you may want to use the Student Self-Assessment form to help you conduct a student-teacher interview. While questioning students and recording their responses, you can help them to better understand your learning goals and you can also help them to develop some of their own. Students in grades three through six can complete the form on their own once they are familiar with all of the expectations. Make sure that they tell you why they gave themselves certain ratings in the circle space provided.

Examples

Primary Grades

A first-grade teacher interviewed a student after he completed a personal time line comprised of photographs and captions. Once completed, the organizer was attached to his time line and added to his portfolio.

Intermediate Grades

A sixth-grade student completed this self-evaluation at the completion of the first trimester. The form accompanied her report card home.

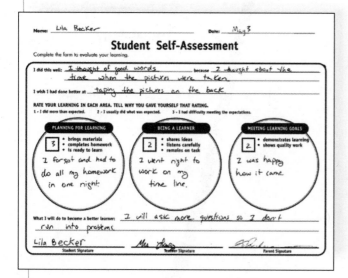

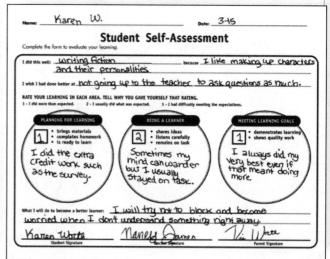

Name: _____   Date: _____

Student Self-Assessment

Complete the form to evaluate your learning.

I did this well: _____

I wish I had done better at _____ because _____

RATE YOUR LEARNING IN EACH AREA. TELL WHY YOU GAVE YOURSELF THAT RATING.

1 - I did more than expected.   2 - I usually did what was expected.   3 - I had difficulty meeting the expectations.

PLANNING FOR LEARNING

☐

- brings materials
- completes homework
- is ready to learn

BEING A LEARNER

☐

- shares ideas
- listens carefully
- remains on task

MEETING LEARNING GOALS

☐

- demonstrates learning
- shows quality work

What I will do to become a better learner: _____

_____   _____   _____
Student Signature   Teacher Signature   Parent Signature

MY PORTFOLIO

⁺✦ Skills

Students will:

+ **meet criteria for performance evaluation**

+ **identify characteristic examples of schoolwork**

+ **develop skills of self-evaluation**

Purpose

Portfolios are collections of student work designed to show the growth of the student's knowledge and skills. When used properly, they can be rich assessment tools that provide students, parents, and teachers with a great deal of information about a student's performance. In order for this assessment process to work effectively, students must actively participate in selecting and evaluating the contents of the portfolio. This graphic organizer gives students a means for keeping track of their portfolio selections. In addition, the organizer asks that students reflect and evaluate the material they have chosen.

How to Use the Organizer

To introduce portfolio assessment and the graphic organizer to students, explain that a portfolio is a work in progress. Tell students that although their portfolios should include examples of their best work, they should also include work samples that show progress. To underscore the point, hold up a handwriting example from the beginning of the year or (as timing dictates) the previous year. Compare the example with a current sample of the same person's handwriting. Point out that students can only see the improvement in handwriting by seeing both examples side by side. In the early grades, you may have to record students' opinions and observations. In the upper grades, both teacher and student may have a hand in selecting and evaluating portfolio materials.

Examples

Primary Grades

A second grader selected works from her mathematics class and recorded her impressions of each piece on the organizer. During October conferences, the students' parents leafed through the portfolio, asking questions about specific selections and commending their child for progress shown.

Intermediate Grades

A fifth-grade teacher asked students to help her collect materials for their performance portfolios. In general, the teacher gave her students full reign in selecting and evaluating materials. In this case, however, the teacher asked that students include one writing sample from the beginning of the term and another later in the term.

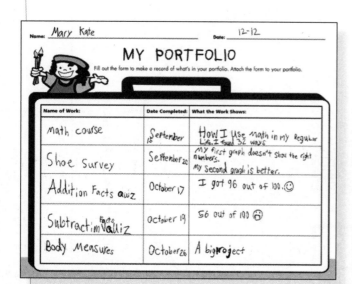

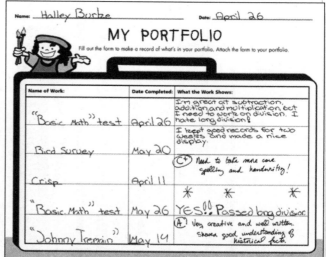

Name: _____

MY PORTFOLIO

Fill out the form to make a record of what's in your portfolio. Attach the form to your portfolio.

Name of Work:	Date Completed:	What the Work Shows:

PROJECT PLANNING PYRAMIDS

Purpose

The Project Planning Pyramids help students to conceptualize an independent project from beginning to evaluation. If students are working cooperatively, it provides a forum for discussing how the plan will be developed and what role students will take.

How to Use the Organizer

Once you have presented your criteria for a project, invite students to use this organizer to help them develop their ideas. Suggest that they decide on a topic and record it in the first pyramid. Allow them time to do some preliminary research and discuss their ideas before completing the rest of the graphic. If a student has difficulty coming up with resources or materials, or if the topic does not lend itself to a demonstration, suggest that the student explore one of the other topics suggested and complete a new organizer.

Skills

Students will:

+ choose an appropriate topic

+ investigate ways to conduct research

+ organize information to create, complete, and evaluate the project

Examples

Primary Grades

A third-grade teacher asked her class to conduct research on a constellation using three different print resources. The children demonstrated what they learned by creating a fact web and by sharing a mythical legend.

Intermediate Grades

A team of sixth graders chose to study Egypt for their Ancient Civilization project. With their combined experiences, they came up with a unique way of involving the class in their presentation.

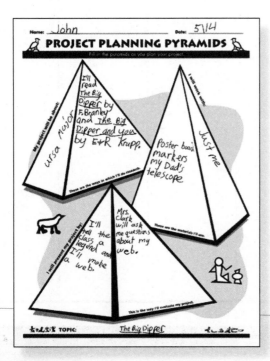

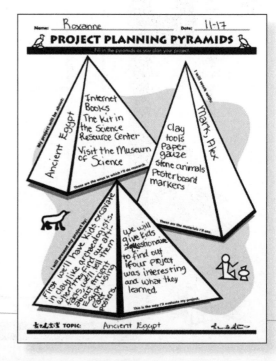

Name: _____   Date: _____

 # PROJECT PLANNING PYRAMIDS

Fill in the pyramids as you plan your project.

My project will be about:

I will work with:

These are the ways in which I'll do research.

I will present my project by:

These are the materials I'll use.

This is the way I'll evaluate my project.

TOPIC:

HOMEWORK MACHINE

Skills

Students will:

+ **record weekly assignments**

+ **gain experience in managing their own time**

+ **communicate necessary information at home**

Purpose

Learning to look ahead and to manage one's time well takes a good deal of practice. The Homework Machine organizer helps students develop a greater sense of control over their independent time and responsibilities. It reminds them to balance their time between daily obligations and long-term projects. It also gives parents a place to look to make sure that they are receiving all the important notices that come from you.

How to Use the Organizer

You may want to allot some time each Monday to completing this organizer. This will give you an opportunity to reinforce due dates and to remind students of procedures. Or, you can fill in the organizer and photocopy it for students on a weekly basis. To individualize the completion of this organizer, have students keep a copy in their homework folder and remind them when they need to add an assignment or change a date. Or post a list of questions for students to answer such as, "Have you completed your artwork?" As they answer the questions, they can include necessary information on their form. The "Notes to show" section reminds students to deliver all messages from you or other school personnel to the appropriate person at home.

Examples

Primary Grades

A first-grade teacher had her students complete this organizer to help them (and their parents) keep track of the days that they had added responsibilities.

Intermediate Grades

Knowing the week's assignments helped fourth-grade students work around extracurricular activities and family plans. Assignments could be done ahead of time, and long-range projects were less apt to be left until the last evening.

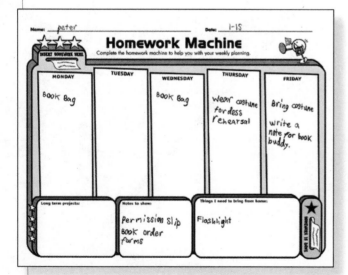

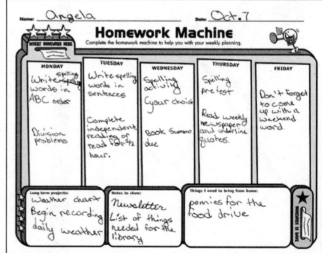

Name: _____

Date: _____

Homework Machine

Complete the homework machine to help you with your weekly planning.

INSERT HOMEWORK HERE

MONDAY

TUESDAY

WEDNESDAY

THURSDAY

FRIDAY

HOMEWORK IS DONE

Long term projects:

Notes to show:

Things I need to bring from home:

TEST AHEAD!

Purpose

Of the many forms of assessment available to educators today, testing is still the most common. Throughout their school careers, students will face many different kinds of tests, from the simplest quiz on addition facts to high-stakes national standardized tests. Students often fail to do well on tests, not because they do not know the material, but because they do not know how to approach a test. The steps listed in the Test Ahead! study guide are applicable to most subject areas and offer strategies both for studying and for taking tests.

How to Use the Organizer

How you present this organizer will depend upon what kind of test your students are about to take. Primary students have few tests that require advanced preparation; however, they can benefit from the general suggestions in the "Prepare" and "Pounce" sections when preparing to take state- or district-mandated standardized tests. For older students who will be taking teacher-prepared tests, hand out the organizer early in the year or unit of study. Read through and discuss the steps listed in each section.

✦ Skills

Students will:

✦ become acquainted with test-taking strategies

✦ develop strong study habits

Examples

Primary Grades

A class of second graders were about to take their first standardized reading test. The teacher checked the items on the organizer that applied to her students and distributed copies to the class. When notices announcing the standardized tests went home to parents, she attached copies of the organizer, with a note of explanation about the tests and the appropriate preparation steps checked.

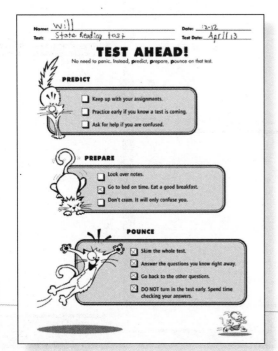

Intermediate Grades

To prepare his fifth graders for middle school curriculum, a science teacher incorporated the use of science textbooks and unit tests into his own curriculum. Throughout the year, at the beginning of each new unit, he reviewed the organizer. Once students were familiar with the steps of test preparation, the teacher distributed copies to students *after* the test, so that they could use the organizer to self-evaluate their test-taking skills.

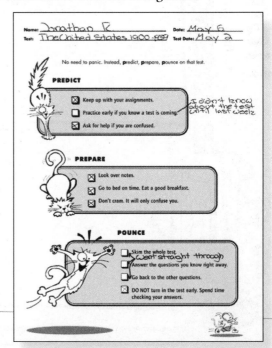

Name: _____   Date: _____

Test: _____   Test Date: _____

TEST AHEAD!

No need to panic. Instead, **p**redict, **p**repare, **p**ounce on that test.

PREDICT

- [ ] Keep up with your assignments.
- [ ] Practice early if you know a test is coming.
- [ ] Ask for help if you are confused.

PREPARE

- [ ] Look over notes.
- [ ] Go to bed on time. Eat a good breakfast.
- [ ] Don't cram. It will only confuse you.

POUNCE

- [ ] Skim the whole test.
- [ ] Answer the questions you know right away.
- [ ] Go back to the other questions.
- [ ] DO NOT turn in the test early. Spend time checking your answers.

★ MANY HANDS MAKE LIGHT WORK

✦✦ Skills

Students will:

✦ **plan a group activity**

✦ **identify tasks required to complete an activity**

✦ **designate roles for group members**

Purpose

Working within cooperative learning groups allows students to take responsibility for planning an activity and designating roles, and to practice the skills of social interaction. Cooperative groups can use this organizer to record tasks and responsibilities and develop a plan of action for completing an assigned project.

How to Use the Organizer

Before students divide into small groups, review the procedure for completing the organizer. Groups of older students can designate one person to record the information on the chart. A teacher or adult volunteer can work with younger groups to complete the chart and guide the activity.

Examples

Primary Grades

A parent volunteer worked with small groups of first graders to make "fish fossil" prints. Before beginning the project, the volunteer read through the organizer and asked group members to help her complete the chart. The teacher asked that students follow the same procedure whenever they worked in small groups. By the end of the year, all students were well acquainted with the process of planning a group activity, and many could fill in the chart for their group on their own.

Intermediate Grades

Sixth graders worked in pairs to perform a controlled science experiment. They used the organizer to plan and record the steps of their experiment and to clarify task assignments. To emphasize the importance of the planning stage of an experiment, the teacher checked that each group had completed the chart before allowing them to proceed with the experiment. Students understood that part of their final grade on the project was based on their ability to work cooperatively as a group.

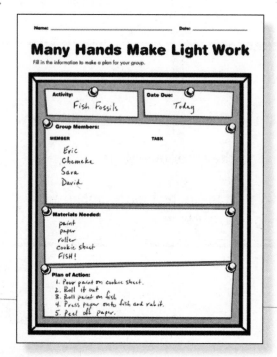

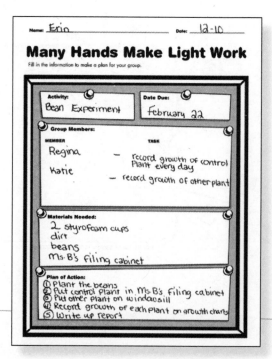

Name: _____ Date: _____

Many Hands Make Light Work

Fill in the information to make a plan for your group.

Activity:

Date Due:

Group Members:

MEMBER   TASK

Materials Needed:

Plan of Action:

★ PLAN, PRACTICE, AND PRESENT

✦ Skills

Students will:

✦ **plan and present an oral report**

✦ **develop research and study skills**

Purpose

Many of the skills students need for organizing an oral report are similar to those required for writing a basic research report. Often, however, students are not taught the organizational skills that are unique to oral presentations. This organizer provides an outline for planning, practicing, and presenting any kind of oral presentation and will help students gain skill and confidence in public speaking.

How to Use the Organizer

Distribute copies of the organizer and review with students the steps listed in each section. As students prepare their oral presentations, have them check each step they complete. With inexperienced students, you may want to have the whole class complete one step at a time. As students gain experience in the process of preparing an oral presentation, they can begin to work at their own pace.

To use the organizer as an assessment tool, highlight the steps listed in the "Plan" and "Present" sections that you would like to use as performance objectives. Check off each objective that the student has met in the course of planning and presenting his oral presentation.

Examples

Primary Grades

Once a month, each student in a third-grade class was required to give a brief oral presentation on an independent reading book. At the beginning of the year, the teacher handed out the oral presentation checklist and, using a book she had read to the class as an example, modeled the steps listed on the organizer. She asked students to keep copies of the organizer in their reading folders and throughout the year she reviewed the checklist with individual students during reading conferences.

Intermediate Grades

A class of sixth graders worked in study teams to prepare oral presentations on research topics of their choice. Pairs of students used the suggestions listed on the organizer to plan their presentations and conduct practice sessions before giving their presentations before the class.

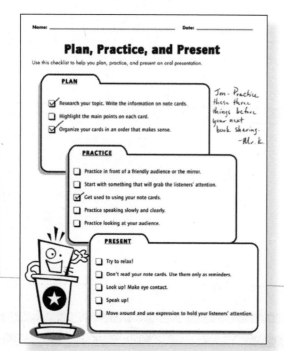

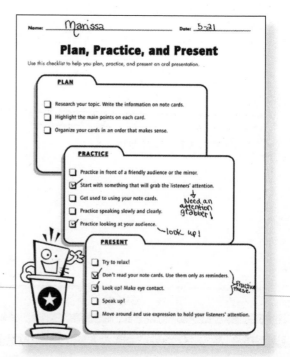

Plan, Practice, and Present

Use this checklist to help you plan, practice, and present an oral presentation.

PLAN

- ☐ Research your topic. Write the information on note cards.
- ☐ Highlight the main points on each card.
- ☐ Organize your cards in an order that makes sense.

PRACTICE

- ☐ Practice in front of a friendly audience or the mirror.
- ☐ Start with something that will grab the listeners' attention.
- ☐ Get used to using your note cards.
- ☐ Practice speaking slowly and clearly.
- ☐ Practice looking at your audience.

PRESENT

- ☐ Try to relax!
- ☐ Don't read your note cards. Use them only as reminders.
- ☐ Look up! Make eye contact.
- ☐ Speak up!
- ☐ Move around and use expression to hold your listeners' attention.

INTERVIEWING GUIDE

Skills

Students will:

+ plan and conduct an interview

+ identify key questions to ask interview subjects

Purpose

Interviewing is an important research method—one that is too often over-looked in the elementary curriculum. In order to obtain the information they need, the students must plan carefully and conduct the interview properly. The Interviewing Guide provides guidelines for both planning and conducting interviews. Students can use the guide to help them prepare their questions and to remind them of important interviewing procedures.

How to Use the Organizer

To introduce the organizer, ask students to describe interviews that they have read or seen on TV. Discuss the types of people who are usually interviewed in the media (sports figures, political candidates, celebrities) and ask students to name people that they would like to interview if they had the opportunity. For each interviewee named, ask students to suggest questions that they would like to ask. Tell them that the Interviewing Guide will help them plan their interviews.

Another way to use this organizer is as a recording devise for fictitious interviews with historical or literary figures. Students choose appropriate times and places for the interview, and write both the interviewer's questions and the subject's answers.

Examples

Primary Grades

First graders were asked to interview a family member. One first grader conducted the interview with his grandmother in Spanish. His mother translated the questions, and recorded the answers in English on the Interviewing Guide. The teacher asked for a picture of each interviewee, and posted the pictures and interviews on a bulletin board entitled "Family Stories."

Intermediate Grades

For independent reading, a fourth grader read Roald Dahl's *Matilda*. Instead of writing an entry in his response journal, he chose to conduct an imaginary interview with Matilda—just one of many options his teacher had made available for responding to books.

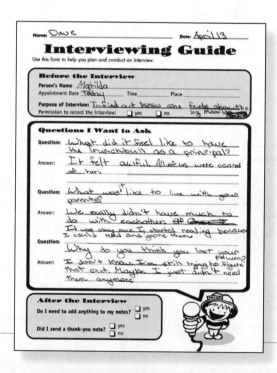

Name: _____ Date: _____

Interviewing Guide
Use this form to help you plan and conduct an interview.

Before the Interview

Person's Name _____

Appointment Date _____ Time_____ Place _____

Purpose of Interview: _____

Permission to record the interview: ☐ yes ☐ no

Questions I Want to Ask

Question: _____
_____

Answer: _____
_____
_____

Question: _____
_____

Answer: _____
_____
_____

Question: _____
_____

Answer: _____
_____
_____

After the Interview

Do I need to add anything to my notes? ☐ yes ☐ no

Did I send a thank-you note? ☐ yes ☐ no

READING RECORD

Skills

Students will:

+ identify literary genres

+ evaluate written material

+ draw conclusions based on their record keeping

Purpose

The Reading Record form not only gives children a place to record reading selections, it also asks them to identify the genres they choose and to chart their own reading patterns. Teachers may establish criteria for using the form such as "comment on character change in the story," or "choose from at least three different genres."

How to Use the Organizer

Introduce this record-keeping form after children have had experience in identifying different literary genres. Ask children to record the date, title, and author, and the number for the type of book on the form. Some children may have difficulty recording genre, since a book can be both fantasy and humorous. To help children choose a number, suggest that they think of the author's purpose for writing the book. If the genre is still not clear, you may want to have children look up the Library of Congress classification or simply have them record more than one number in the box provided. Students can write general impressions in the comment section, or you might suggest that they answer a particular question when responding.

Examples

Primary Grades

A third-grade teacher identified a student's reading and response patterns, and guided her toward longer works by helping her find chapter books that had brave female protagonists and/or compassion for animals.

Intermediate Grades

Fifth graders were asked to record and evaluate their at-home reading. They were required to read a variety of books—at least four different genres for each reading form.

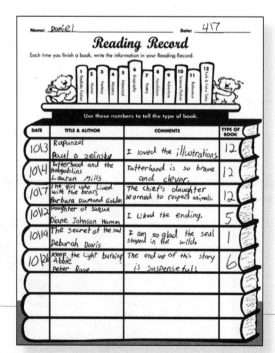

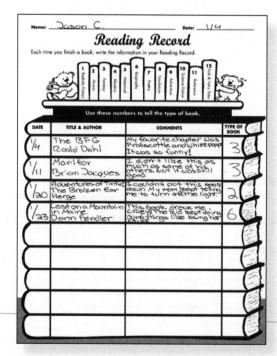

Reading Record

Each time you finish a book, write the information in your Reading Record.

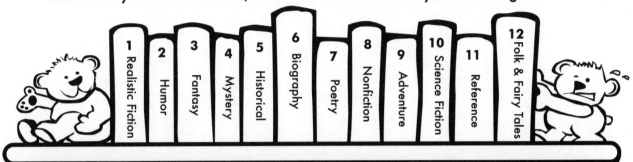

1 Realistic Fiction
2 Humor
3 Fantasy
4 Mystery
5 Historical
6 Biography
7 Poetry
8 Nonfiction
9 Adventure
10 Science Fiction
11 Reference
12 Folk & Fairy Tales

Use these numbers to tell the type of book.

DATE	TITLE & AUTHOR	COMMENTS	TYPE OF BOOK